CW00410392

NEBRASKA TRAVEL GUIDE 2023

An Updated Traveler's Manual to Historic Trails, Unique Experiences and Local Delights in Nebraska, Packed with Insider Tips and Local Recommendations

CARL OWEN

Copyright © 2023 by Carl Owen

All rights reserved. No part of this travel guide book, titled "Exploring Nebraska: Uncovering the Heartland's Hidden Gems," may be reproduced, distributed, or transmitted in any form or by any means, including photocopying, recording, or other electronic or mechanical methods, without the prior written permission of the publisher, except in the case of brief quotations embodied in critical reviews and certain other non-commercial uses permitted by copyright law.

TABLE OF CONTENTS

CHAPTER 3: EXPLORING OMAHA

CHAPTER 4: LINCOLN - NEBRASKA'S CAPITAL

CHAPTER 6: THE GREAT PLAINS AND SANDHILLS

CHAPTER 7: EASTERN NEBRASKA GEMS

CHAPTER 8: OUTDOOR ADVENTURES

CHAPTER 9: NEBRASKA'S HIDDEN TREASURES

CHAPTER 10: CULINARY DELIGHTS

CHAPTER 11: FAMILY-FRIENDLY FUN

CHAPTER 12: PRACTICALITIES

CHAPTER 13: TRAVELING NEBRASKA ON A BUDGET

CHAPTER 14: LANGUAGE AND CULTURE

CHAPTER 15: NEBRASKA SOUVENIRS AND MEMENTOS

INTRODUCTION

In the vast expanse of the American heartland lies the enchanting state of Nebraska, a land of rolling plains and warm hospitality. I had the privilege of discovering this gem during my first visit, an experience that forever changed my life and brought me unexpected joys.

As I stepped off the plane at Omaha's Eppley Airfield, my excitement was tinged with a hint of nervousness. Exploring a new state on my own seemed both thrilling and daunting. Armed with my travel guide and a backpack filled with anticipation, I set out to unravel the wonders Nebraska had to offer.

Little did I know that fate had something extraordinary in store for me that day. As I stood in the bustling airport, trying to decipher the labyrinthine map of the city, a friendly voice called out, "Are you new in town? Need a hand?"

Turning around, I met the warmest smile I had ever seen. It belonged to a woman named Sarah. Her eyes sparkled with kindness, and her aura exuded a genuine sense of compassion. I gladly accepted her offer of help, and she guided me through the intricacies of Omaha with ease.

Over the next few days, Sarah became my newfound friend and invaluable guide. She introduced me to the hidden treasures of Nebraska, from the stunning Platte River to the majestic Scotts Bluff National Monument. As we strolled through quaint towns and vibrant cities, our laughter resonated through the plains, creating unforgettable memories.

As our friendship grew deeper, we discovered shared passions and interests. Our conversations flowed effortlessly, and we soon realized that our souls connected on a profound level. In each other's company, we felt a sense of belonging and comfort, as if we had known each other for a lifetime.

Months turned into years, and Sarah and I found ourselves inseparable. We experienced the changing seasons of Nebraska together, marveling at the vivid colors of autumn and relishing the sweet summer sunsets. Love blossomed between us, and we embarked on a journey of love, commitment, and shared dreams.

One day, as we gazed at the Nebraska sky, we made a decision that would forever shape our lives. We wanted to build a family together, to nurture a new generation amidst the very beauty that brought us together. Our love flourished, and soon enough, we welcomed two adorable bundles of joy into our lives, the embodiment of our love and the next chapter of our extraordinary adventure.

Nebraska, with its charm and serendipity, had given us the most unexpected gift - a family bound by love and rooted in the heart of the heartland. The land of open skies had opened its arms to embrace us, making our story a testament to the wonders that await those who embark on their own Nebraska journey.

As you plan your own adventure in Nebraska, fellow travelers, be prepared for surprises beyond your wildest imagination. Keep your eyes open for the unexpected friendships that may bloom and the life-changing encounters that might come your way. Nebraska is not just a destination; it's an experience that has the power to touch your heart and change your life forever.

In this guide, 5 chapters ranging from chapter 3 to chapter 7 are dedicated to discussing 5 major cities and regions of Nebraska, namely, Omaha (The largest city in Nebraska), Lincoln (The state's capital), Western Nebraska, The great plains and sandhills and finally, Eastern Nebraska.

So, with heads held high and hearts full of anticipation, set forth on your Nebraska expedition. Embrace the spirit of adventure, and let the warm winds of the plains carry you towards the unforgettable moments that await you. Let Nebraska be the backdrop of your own unique tale, one that you'll cherish for a lifetime.

CHAPTER 1: WELCOME TO NEBRASKA

1.1 WHY VISIT NEBRASKA

Here are some of the reasons why people consider Nebraska a must visit destination and why others should also consider making this enchanting state their target for a vacation.

People visit Nebraska for its diverse attractions and unique experiences. Nature enthusiasts explore its vast prairies, stunning sandhills, and scenic rivers, offering opportunities for outdoor activities like hiking, birdwatching, and fishing. History buffs are drawn to its rich pioneer heritage, with attractions like the Oregon Trail and Chimney Rock.

For those seeking cultural experiences, Nebraska offers vibrant cities like Omaha and Lincoln, boasting museums, art galleries, and lively festivals. The warm hospitality of the locals and affordable travel costs make Nebraska an inviting destination for all.

People should consider visiting Nebraska to discover its hidden gems, immerse in its welcoming atmosphere, and experience a mix of natural beauty and cultural charm that sets it apart from other travel destinations.

1.2 GEOGRAPHICAL LOCATION AND CLIMATE OF NEBRASKA

Geographical Location:

Nebraska is a state located in the Midwestern region of the United States. It is bordered by six other states: South Dakota to the north, Iowa to the east, Missouri to the southeast, Kansas to the south, Colorado to the southwest, and Wyoming to the west. The state's total area spans approximately 77,354 square miles (200,520 square kilometers), making it the 16th largest state in the U.S.

The Missouri River runs along Nebraska's eastern border, providing an important waterway for transportation and irrigation. The state's landscape is characterized by vast prairies, rolling plains, and fertile farmland, earning it the nickname "The Cornhusker State."

Climate:

Nebraska experiences a continental climate, with distinct four seasons and relatively low humidity throughout much of the year. The state's climate is influenced by its inland location and the absence of major geographical barriers to the movement of air masses.

Summer (June to August): Summers in Nebraska are typically hot and humid. Average high temperatures range from 85°F to 95°F (29°C to 35°C), but can occasionally reach well over 100°F (38°C) during heatwaves.

Thunderstorms are common during this season, providing much-needed moisture for agriculture.

Autumn (September to November): Fall brings milder temperatures and beautiful foliage as the leaves change color. Average highs in September start around 80°F (27°C) and drop to the mid-50s°F (around 12°C) by November.

Winter (December to February): Winters in Nebraska can be quite cold, especially in the northern parts of the state. Average temperatures in December range from the mid-30s°F (around 2°C) in the south to the mid-20s°F (around -4°C) in the north. Snowfall is common during the winter months, providing opportunities for winter sports and activities.

Spring (March to May): Spring is a transitional season with rapidly changing weather. Average highs in March start in the mid-40s°F (around 7°C) and rise to the mid-60s°F (around 18°C) in May. Springtime in Nebraska can bring severe weather, including thunderstorms, tornadoes, and occasional flooding.

Due to its continental climate, Nebraska can experience temperature extremes, with cold snaps in winter and heatwaves in summer. This variability can pose challenges to agriculture, but it also contributes to the state's rich biodiversity and abundant wildlife.

Overall, Nebraska's geographical location and climate play a significant role in shaping its landscapes, economy, and the daily lives of its residents.

1.3 SIGNIFICANT HISTORICAL PERIODS OF NEBRASKA

Nebraska has a rich history that encompasses various significant historical periods. Here are some of the most noteworthy periods in Nebraska's history:

Indigenous Peoples: Before European settlement, Nebraska was inhabited by various indigenous peoples, including the Omaha, Pawnee, Ponca, and Lakota Sioux. These Native American tribes lived off the land, engaging in hunting, agriculture, and trade.

Westward Expansion: With the Louisiana Purchase in 1803, the region that would become Nebraska came under American control. The

Oregon Trail, the California Trail, and other routes passed through Nebraska during the 19th century, bringing pioneers and settlers seeking new opportunities and a better life in the West.

Nebraska Territory: In 1854, the Kansas-Nebraska Act established the Nebraska Territory, which initially included present-day Nebraska and parts of surrounding states. This period saw tensions between pro-slavery and anti-slavery factions, as Nebraska was at the center of the national debate over the expansion of slavery.

Statehood: Nebraska was admitted as the 37th state of the United States on March 1, 1867. Statehood marked a new era for Nebraska, with its capital city, Lincoln, named after the 16th

President of the United States, Abraham Lincoln.

Agricultural Development: Nebraska's fertile soil and favorable climate made it a prime location for agricultural development. During the late 19th and early 20th centuries, the state's economy thrived on farming and livestock production, earning it the nickname "The Cornhusker State."

Transcontinental Railroad: The completion of the First Transcontinental Railroad in 1869 was a transformative event for Nebraska. The railroad connected the east and west coasts of the United States, leading to increased trade, population growth, and the establishment of new towns and cities along the railway.

Great Depression and Dust Bowl: Nebraska, like much of the country, experienced significant hardships during the Great Depression of the 1930s. The state was also affected by the Dust Bowl, a severe drought and soil erosion crisis that caused widespread agricultural devastation.

Civil Rights Movement: During the mid-20th century, Nebraska played a role in the civil rights movement. Activists worked to address racial discrimination and promote equality, and Nebraska was one of the early states to pass fair housing legislation.

Modern Development: In the post-World War II era, Nebraska experienced continued growth and development. The state's economy diversified, with the expansion of industries such as manufacturing, finance, and services.

These significant historical periods have shaped Nebraska into the vibrant and diverse state it is today, with a strong sense of heritage and an eye towards the future.

CHAPTER 2: PLANNING YOUR TRIP

2.1 BEST TIME TO VISIT

The best time to visit Nebraska is during the spring and fall seasons, which typically span from April to June and September to October, respectively. During these months, the weather is mild and pleasant, with comfortable temperatures ranging from 50°F to 70°F (10°C to 25°C). Springtime brings beautiful blooming flowers and rejuvenated landscapes, while autumn displays stunning foliage colors, making it an ideal time for outdoor activities and sightseeing.

If you prefer warmer weather and want to engage in various recreational opportunities, summer can also be a good time to visit. From June to August, the temperatures range from 75°F to 90°F (24°C to 32°C), making it suitable for exploring Nebraska's scenic lakes, enjoying water sports, and attending lively local festivals.

Winter, from December to February, can be harsh with temperatures ranging from 15°F to 35°F (-9°C to 2°C) and occasional snowfall. However, if you enjoy winter sports like skiing or want a quieter and more budget-friendly experience, this season could be a unique time to explore the state.

Keep in mind that Nebraska's weather can be unpredictable, so it's always advisable to check the local forecasts before planning your trip. Regardless of the season, Nebraska offers diverse attractions, including the Sandhills,

Chimney Rock, Omaha's cultural scene, and the fascinating wildlife at the Platte River during migration seasons, ensuring a memorable experience year-round.

2.2 VISA REQUIREMENTS AND ENTRY REGULATIONS

Nebraska, like all states in the United States, follows federal visa requirements and entry regulations. For international travelers planning to visit Nebraska, it's essential to understand the visa and entry guidelines to ensure a smooth and hassle-free trip.

Visa Requirements: Visitors from foreign countries typically require a visa to enter the

United States, unless they come from a visa waiver program country. The visa category needed depends on the purpose of the visit, such as tourism, business, study, or work.

Visa Waiver Program (VWP): Citizens of countries participating in the Visa Waiver Program can enter the United States for tourism or business purposes without obtaining a visa. However, they must apply for an Electronic System for Travel Authorization (ESTA) before traveling.

B-1/B-2 Visitor Visa: Travelers who do not qualify for the VWP may apply for a B-1 visa (business) or B-2 visa (tourism) at a U.S. embassy or consulate in their home country.

Visa Application Process: Applicants need to submit the necessary documents, attend an interview, and pay the visa fee. Processing times may vary, so it's advisable to apply well in advance of the planned travel date.

ESTA: For VWP travelers, the ESTA application is an online process that determines eligibility to enter the U.S. It is recommended to apply for ESTA at least 72 hours before departure.

Port of Entry: Upon arrival in Nebraska, travelers must go through the U.S. Customs and Border Protection (CBP) at a designated port of entry. CBP officers will inspect documents and determine the length of stay allowed.

Passport Validity: All travelers must have a valid passport for the duration of their stay. The passport should have at least six months of validity beyond the intended departure date from the U.S.

Visa Extension: If travelers wish to extend their stay beyond the visa expiration date, they must apply for an extension with the U.S. Citizenship and Immigration Services (USCIS).

Visa Waiver for Canada and Bermuda: Canadian and Bermudian citizens do not need a visa to enter the U.S. for short visits but must have a valid passport.

Work Visa: Individuals seeking employment in Nebraska must obtain an appropriate work visa, such as an H-1B, L-1, or O-1 visa, depending on their qualifications and job offer.

Student Visa: International students planning to study in Nebraska should apply for an F-1 or M-1 student visa, depending on their course of study.

Visa Overstays: It is crucial to adhere to the authorized length of stay. Overstaying can result in serious consequences, including future visa denials.

For the most accurate and up-to-date information on visa requirements and entry regulations in Nebraska, travelers should consult the official websites of the U.S. Department of State and U.S. Customs and Border Protection. Proper preparation and compliance with these regulations will ensure a pleasant and trouble-free experience when visiting the beautiful state of Nebraska.

2.3 ACCOMMODATION OPTIONS

Nebraska offers a diverse range of accommodation options to cater to the needs of every traveler. Whether you're exploring the bustling cities or the tranquil countryside, you'll find comfortable places to stay.

Hotels: Nebraska boasts a variety of hotels, from budget-friendly chains to luxurious resorts. Major cities like Omaha and Lincoln offer numerous options with modern amenities and convenient locations.

Motels: Along highways and in smaller towns, you'll find cozy motels that provide affordable overnight stays for travelers passing through or exploring the state.

Bed and Breakfasts: For a more intimate experience, charming bed and breakfasts are scattered throughout Nebraska, offering personalized service and a taste of local hospitality.

Guest Ranches: Experience the true essence of the Midwest at guest ranches, where you can engage in activities like horseback riding and immerse yourself in the rural lifestyle.

Vacation Rentals: Visitors seeking a home-away-from-home experience can opt for vacation rentals, ranging from cabins in the woods to stylish apartments in urban centers.

Campgrounds: Nature enthusiasts can enjoy camping in Nebraska's numerous campgrounds, from state parks to national forests, offering picturesque settings and outdoor adventures.

Resorts: Indulge in luxury at resorts located near beautiful lakes or golf courses, providing relaxation and recreational opportunities.

Boutique Inns: Discover unique boutique inns, often housed in historic buildings, offering a blend of elegance and character.

University Housing: Some universities open their dormitories to visitors during the summer months, providing a budget-friendly option for travelers.

Eco-Lodges: Nebraska's ecotourism scene includes eco-lodges that allow you to connect with nature while supporting sustainable practices.

Casino Hotels: For a touch of excitement, casino hotels in certain areas offer entertainment, dining, and gaming options.

Retreat Centers: Spiritual retreat centers nestled in serene landscapes offer a tranquil escape from the hustle and bustle.

Cabins and Cottages: Enjoy a rustic experience in secluded cabins or cottages, perfect for unwinding and reconnecting with nature.

Extended-Stay Hotels: Ideal for business travelers or those in need of temporary housing, extended-stay hotels provide additional amenities for longer stays.

RV Parks: Travelers with recreational vehicles will find plenty of RV parks with full hookups and facilities for a comfortable stay.

No matter where you choose to stay in Nebraska, the warmth and hospitality of the locals, combined with the state's natural beauty, promise an unforgettable experience for all travelers.

2.4 TRANSPORTATION IN NEBRASKA

The state's transportation infrastructure is well-developed and efficiently connects its cities and rural areas. Here are some of the transportation options available in Nebraska:

Roads and Highways: Nebraska boasts an extensive network of well-maintained roads and highways, making traveling by car or motorcycle a popular choice for both short commutes and long-distance journeys.

Interstate System: Nebraska is intersected by several major interstate highways, including I-80, which runs east-west and serves as a critical corridor for cross-country travel.

Public Transit: Major cities like Omaha and Lincoln provide public transit services with buses and light rail systems, facilitating convenient commuting within urban areas.

Air Travel: Nebraska is served by several regional airports, with the Eppley Airfield in Omaha and the Lincoln Airport offering domestic and regional flights, ensuring easy access to other parts of the country.

Railways: Freight trains play a crucial role in transporting goods across Nebraska, contributing to the state's economy and connectivity to national markets.

Amtrak: Amtrak's California Zephyr route connects Omaha and other cities in Nebraska to Chicago and the West Coast, providing scenic and leisurely travel options.

Bicycle-Friendly: Many urban areas in Nebraska are bicycle-friendly, with dedicated bike lanes and paths, encouraging eco-friendly transportation and promoting a healthy lifestyle.

Ride-Sharing: Ride-sharing services like Uber and Lyft are available in larger cities, offering convenient and flexible transportation solutions.

Car Rentals: Car rental services are easily accessible throughout the state, allowing visitors to explore Nebraska's picturesque landscapes at their own pace.

Greyhound Bus: The Greyhound bus service operates in Nebraska, providing an affordable and long-distance option for intercity travel.

Trucking Industry: Nebraska's strategic location and excellent road connections make it a significant hub for the trucking industry, facilitating the efficient movement of goods.

River Transportation: Nebraska is bordered by the Missouri River, and while not widely used for passenger transport, it plays a vital role in shipping goods.

Charter Services: Various charter companies offer customized transportation services for groups and events, providing a convenient and tailored travel experience.

Air Ambulance: In emergency situations, air ambulance services are available to swiftly transport patients to specialized medical facilities.

Rural Transportation: For residents in rural areas, community-based transportation services are often provided, ensuring access to essential services and healthcare.

In conclusion, Nebraska offers a comprehensive range of transportation options, combining modern roadways, air travel, and public transit, making it easy for residents and tourists to navigate the state efficiently and comfortably. Whether you prefer urban convenience or rural charm, Nebraska has transportation solutions to suit every need.

CHAPTER 3: EXPLORING OMAHA

3.1 OVERVIEW OF OMAHA

Omaha, the largest city in the state of Nebraska, USA, provides a captivating blend of Midwestern charm and modern urban amenities. Situated along the banks of the Missouri River, this vibrant city serves as a cultural and economic hub for the region. With a rich history dating back to its pioneer days, Omaha has grown into a dynamic metropolis known for its friendly residents and diverse attractions.

The city boasts an array of cultural landmarks and museums, such as the Joslyn Art Museum, The Durham Museum, and the Henry Doorly Zoo and Aquarium - one of the finest zoos in the world. Additionally, the historic Old Market district lures visitors with its cobblestone streets, art galleries, boutiques, and a plethora of dining options.

Omaha is also renowned for its strong ties to the music and entertainment industry, having produced numerous influential musicians and hosting a variety of festivals and concerts year-round. Sports enthusiasts can cheer on the Omaha Storm Chasers, the city's Triple-A baseball team, or experience the electrifying college sports scene.

The city's economy thrives on a diverse range of sectors, including finance, telecommunications, healthcare, and agriculture. With its central location in the United States, Omaha serves as a strategic transportation and logistics center, making it a prime destination for businesses and industries.

Nature enthusiasts can find solace in the city's parks and recreational areas, providing ample opportunities for outdoor activities and family outings. Meanwhile, the Riverfront area and Bob Kerrey Pedestrian Bridge present an excellent setting for strolls along the Missouri River.

In summary, Omaha embraces its historical roots while embracing progress and innovation. This inviting city enthralls both residents and visitors alike with its cultural offerings, thriving economy, and warm, welcoming atmosphere.

3.2 TOP ATTRACTIONS IN OMAHA

Here are some of the top attractions that make Omaha a must-visit destination:

Henry Doorly Zoo and Aquarium: One of the world's best zoos, it boasts an impressive collection of animals and a spectacular indoor rainforest.

The Old Market: A historic district filled with cobblestone streets, charming boutiques, art galleries, and a vibrant dining scene.

Lauritzen Gardens: A botanical oasis featuring stunning gardens, water features, and seasonal displays.

Joslyn Art Museum: An architectural marvel with a vast collection of European and American art, including works by Monet and Rembrandt.

Bob Kerrey Pedestrian Bridge: A unique pedestrian bridge spanning the Missouri River, offering picturesque views of the city skyline.

Durham Museum: Housed in a beautifully restored Art Deco train station, it offers captivating exhibits on Omaha's history and transportation.

Heartland of America Park: A serene urban park with a lake, fountains, and a captivating light and water show.

The Durham Museum: Housed in a beautifully restored Art Deco train station, it offers captivating exhibits on Omaha's history and transportation.

Omaha Children's Museum: An interactive and educational wonderland for kids, with hands-on exhibits and activities.

Strategic Air Command & Aerospace Museum: An intriguing museum that showcases historic aircraft and exhibits related to aviation and the Strategic Air Command.

Joslyn Castle: A stunning mansion with elaborate architecture and beautiful gardens, offering guided tours.

Holland Performing Arts Center: A modern venue hosting a variety of performances, including symphonies, concerts, and theatrical productions.

Gene Leahy Mall: A serene urban park in downtown Omaha, complete with walking paths, gardens, and a scenic lagoon.

CenturyLink Center Omaha: A major arena that hosts concerts, sporting events, and entertainment shows.

Stinson Park at Aksarben Village: A lively outdoor venue with concerts, events, and a farmer's market during the summer.

El Museo Latino: The first Latino art and history museum in the Midwest, featuring exhibits from Latin American countries.

Zorinsky Lake Park: A vast recreational area with walking trails, fishing opportunities, and picnic spots.

Fontenelle Forest: A nature lover's paradise with hiking trails, wildlife, and educational programs.

General Crook House Museum: A historic mansion showcasing the life of General George Crook and 19th-century living.

RailsWest Railroad Museum: An engaging museum showcasing the role of the railroad in shaping Omaha's history.

With its rich cultural heritage, impressive attractions, and warm Midwestern hospitality, Omaha offers visitors an unforgettable experience that leaves them wanting to return for more.

3.3 CULTURAL AND ARTISTIC SCENE

The city of Omaha prides itself on it's rich and diverse cultural and artistic scene that captivates residents and visitors alike. With a strong sense of community and a growing population, the city has become a hub for creativity and expression.

The city's art museums, such as the Joslyn Art Museum and the Bemis Center for Contemporary Arts, showcase an impressive collection of both classic and modern works, drawing art enthusiasts from far and wide. Additionally, the Hot Shops Art Center, an exciting creative space, houses numerous local artists' studios, providing an opportunity for visitors to witness art in the making.

Omaha's cultural diversity is celebrated through various events and festivals. The annual Omaha Summer Arts Festival brings together talented artists, musicians, and performers, filling the streets with an atmosphere of excitement and creativity. The Native Omaha Days, a celebration of African-American culture and heritage, showcases art, music, and culinary delights unique to the community.

Music thrives in Omaha, with a thriving indie and alternative scene. The city has produced several renowned bands and musicians, contributing to its reputation as a breeding ground for musical talent. The Slowdown and The Waiting Room Lounge are popular venues that regularly host live performances, fostering a strong sense of musical appreciation among locals.

Theater enthusiasts can revel in the offerings of the Omaha Community Playhouse, a renowned institution that stages a wide range of productions, from classic plays to contemporary works, drawing large audiences of all ages. Moreover, the Omaha Performing Arts Center regularly features Broadway shows and concerts, attracting big-name performers and ensuring a steady stream of top-notch entertainment.

Beyond the traditional arts, Omaha also embraces emerging art forms and technological innovations. Art installations and interactive exhibits can be found in unexpected places throughout the city, encouraging residents and visitors to engage with art in a unique and immersive way.

In conclusion, Omaha's cultural and artistic scene is a tapestry of tradition, innovation, and diversity. With a growing community of artists, musicians, performers, and enthusiasts, the city continues to evolve as a dynamic cultural destination. Whether you're a lover of classic art, contemporary music, or experimental theater, Omaha offers a vibrant and thriving scene that promises something extraordinary for everyone.

3.4 DINING AND NIGHTLIFE

Omaha provides a vibrant and diverse dining and nightlife scene to satisfy every palate and mood.

Whether you're a foodie seeking culinary adventures or looking to unwind after dark, Omaha has something to offer everyone.

Omaha's dining options are a delightful mix of classic American cuisine and international flavors. From upscale restaurants serving prime steaks and farm-to-table delicacies to cozy cafes with locally sourced ingredients, there's no shortage of delicious choices. Don't miss out on trying the renowned Omaha Steaks, a true local specialty that will leave your taste buds wanting more.

As the sun sets, Omaha comes alive with an array of nightlife options. If you're into craft beer and spirits, the city boasts several breweries and distilleries that offer tours and tastings. For those who enjoy live music, Omaha's music venues host a diverse range of performances, from indie bands to big-name artists.

The Old Market district is a must-visit for those seeking a lively atmosphere. Its cobblestone streets are lined with pubs, bars, and restaurants that offer a perfect blend of great food, live entertainment, and a bustling crowd. If you're looking for a more relaxed setting, Omaha's rooftop bars offer stunning views of the city skyline while sipping on cocktails.

For the adventurous, late-night eateries serve up tasty treats that cater to all-night cravings. From gourmet food trucks to 24-hour diners, you won't go hungry even in the early hours.

Omaha's dining and nightlife scene truly encapsulates the city's dynamic spirit. With a mix of flavors, entertainment, and welcoming atmosphere, you're sure to create unforgettable memories as you dine and explore after dark in this charming Midwestern city.

3.5 SHOPPING IN OMAHA

The city of Omaha, provides an exciting shopping experience for both residents and visitors alike. With a diverse array of shopping destinations, this Midwestern gem caters to all tastes and preferences.

The city boasts several shopping districts, each with its unique charm. For a dose of upscale retail therapy, head to the stylish Village Pointe, where high-end boutiques and designer stores line the streets, providing a sophisticated shopping experience. Alternatively, the Old Market district offers a more eclectic vibe, with its cobbled streets and vintage shops, perfect for treasure hunters and collectors.

Omaha is also home to numerous shopping malls, such as Westroads Mall and Oak View Mall, where shoppers can find an extensive range of popular brands and department stores, making it convenient to get all your shopping done under one roof.

If you're a fan of local products and unique finds, don't miss the various farmers' markets and artisanal boutiques scattered throughout the city. These places showcase the creativity and craftsmanship of local artisans, offering everything from handmade jewelry and pottery to delicious homemade treats.

For antique enthusiasts, Omaha's Antique and Collectors' Fair is a must-visit event, bringing together vendors from all over to display their vintage wares and rare collectibles.

Foodies will also find delight in Omaha's shopping scene, as specialty food stores and gourmet markets offer a plethora of local and international delicacies to savor and bring home.

No matter what you're seeking, shopping in Omaha provides an enriching experience that blends modern convenience with a touch of Midwest charm. With friendly locals and a welcoming atmosphere, this city truly captures the essence of a delightful shopping getaway.

CHAPTER 4: LINCOLN - NEBRASKA'S CAPITAL

4.1 AN OVERVIEW OF LINCOLN

Lincoln, the capital city of Nebraska, is a vibrant and historic Midwestern gem. Located in the southeastern part of the state, Lincoln exudes a charming mix of urban amenities and a laid-back, friendly atmosphere. With a population of around 280,000, it strikes a perfect balance between being a bustling city and a close-knit community.

Steeped in history, Lincoln offers visitors and residents a glimpse into the state's past. The Nebraska State Capitol, a magnificent architectural masterpiece, stands tall as a prominent landmark. Its unique design, featuring a 400-foot domed tower, is a sight to behold. Nearby, the University of Nebraska-Lincoln, with its sprawling campus, adds a youthful energy to the city.

Culture and arts thrive in Lincoln, with a range of museums, galleries, and theaters. The Sheldon Museum of Art, known for its extensive American art collection, is a must-visit for art enthusiasts. For those seeking green spaces and relaxation, the Sunken Gardens and Pioneers Park Nature Center provide serene retreats within the city.

Sports lovers find their haven in Lincoln, as it is home to the beloved University of Nebraska Cornhuskers. The university's football team draws thousands of fans to Memorial Stadium on game days, creating an electrifying atmosphere throughout the city.

Lincoln boasts a diverse culinary scene, offering an array of dining options to cater to every taste. From farm-to-table restaurants serving locally sourced ingredients to international eateries, foodies will find plenty to satisfy their palates.

With a strong emphasis on education and innovation, Lincoln nurtures a thriving economy. The city is home to various industries, including technology, healthcare, and manufacturing, contributing to its overall growth and prosperity. Residents of Lincoln take pride in their sense of community and regularly come together for events and festivals. The annual Nebraska State Fair, held in the city, celebrates the state's agricultural heritage and draws visitors from far and wide.

In summary, Lincoln, Nebraska's capital, is a welcoming city that beautifully melds history, culture, and progress. It's warm and inviting atmosphere, coupled with its strong educational institutions and economic opportunities, make it an attractive place to live, visit, and explore.

4.2 HISTORIC LANDMARKS

Lincoln is a city steeped in history, boasting a wealth of historic landmarks that offer a glimpse into its fascinating past. From majestic buildings to iconic sites, here are some of Lincoln's most significant historic landmarks:

Nebraska State Capitol: A true architectural marvel, the Nebraska State Capitol stands tall as an enduring symbol of the state's heritage. Its soaring 400-foot tower and art deco design make it an iconic landmark in Lincoln.

Governor's Mansion: This stately mansion, built in the early 1950s, serves as the official residence of Nebraska's governors. Its elegant design and manicured gardens make it a sight to behold.

Sheldon Museum of Art: Housed in an exquisite limestone building, the Sheldon Museum of Art displays a remarkable collection of American art, representing various periods and styles.

Sunken Gardens: A serene oasis in the heart of the city, the Sunken Gardens is a stunning blend of terraces, fountains, and vibrant floral displays, making it a popular spot for both locals and visitors.

Haymarket District: Once a bustling market, the Haymarket District now preserves its historic charm with cobblestone streets, old brick warehouses, and a vibrant array of shops and restaurants.

University of Nebraska-Lincoln: Founded in 1869, the university's historic campus showcases beautiful buildings, including the iconic Morrill Hall, which holds significance as the oldest building on campus.

Great Plains Art Museum: This museum celebrates the art and culture of the Great Plains region, housing a diverse collection of traditional and contemporary artworks.

Pioneers Park Nature Center: Offering a glimpse into Nebraska's pioneer history, this nature center preserves the region's prairies, woodlands, and wetlands while hosting historic buildings and artifacts.

Frank H. Woods Telephone Museum: A hidden gem for history enthusiasts, this museum exhibits the evolution of telecommunications and houses vintage equipment and memorabilia.

Historic Haymarket Rail Yard: Once a vital part of Lincoln's development, the restored rail yard now serves as a historical attraction with interactive exhibits and fascinating stories of the city's past.

The Ferguson House: Built in the 1870s, this beautifully restored historic house showcases period furniture and artifacts, providing visitors with a glimpse of life in the late 19th century.

Great Plains Black History Museum: Dedicated to preserving and promoting African-American history, this museum features exhibits highlighting the contributions and struggles of black communities in Nebraska.

These historic landmarks in Lincoln not only serve as points of interest but also stand as a testament to the city's rich cultural heritage and the people who have shaped its history over the years. Exploring these sites allows visitors to connect with the past and gain a deeper appreciation for Lincoln's unique identity.

4.3 PARKS AND NATURE

The city of Lincoln boasts an abundance of parks and nature, offering its residents and visitors a refreshing escape into the great outdoors. Known for its scenic beauty and serene landscapes, the city is a haven for nature lovers and outdoor enthusiasts.

One of the most prominent natural gems in Lincoln is Pioneers Park, a sprawling 1,139-acre green oasis that showcases the region's diverse flora and fauna. With its extensive network of hiking and biking trails, picnic areas, and tranquil lakes, Pioneers Park provides ample opportunities for recreational activities and wildlife observation.

For those seeking a more immersive experience with nature, the Sunken Gardens is a must-visit. This stunning floral paradise features vibrant blooms arranged in artistic patterns, creating a captivating and colorful display throughout the year.

Nature lovers can also explore Wilderness Park, a vast 1,475-acre nature reserve on the outskirts of the city. The park's rugged terrain, wooded areas, and meandering creeks offer a perfect setting for hiking, birdwatching, and communing with nature.

Additionally, the city of Lincoln takes pride in its commitment to maintaining green spaces within the urban landscape. Local parks, such as Antelope Park and Holmes Lake Park, provide well-maintained grounds, playgrounds, and serene lake views, making them ideal spots for relaxation and family outings.

Beyond the city parks, residents and visitors can enjoy the picturesque scenery of the Platte River, which runs nearby. The river provides opportunities for kayaking, fishing, and enjoying riverside trails.

Lincoln's dedication to preserving and nurturing its natural assets has created an inviting atmosphere for residents and visitors alike to connect with the outdoors. Whether one seeks tranquility among flowers, excitement on hiking trails, or leisurely activities in city parks, Lincoln has something to offer for everyone who appreciates the beauty of nature.

4.4 DINING AND ENTERTAINMENT

In the bustling city of Lincoln, dining and entertainment come together to create an unforgettable experience for visitors and locals alike. In this charming city, food enthusiasts can embark on a culinary journey that caters to every palate.

Lincoln boasts a diverse range of dining options, from cozy cafes serving artisanal coffee and freshly baked pastries to upscale restaurants offering delectable farm-to-table creations. For those seeking authentic Nebraskan flavors, steakhouses here are second to none, serving mouthwatering cuts of prime beef.

The city's dining scene is complemented by a thriving craft beer and cocktail culture. Local breweries and distilleries showcase their unique blends, inviting patrons to savor the distinct taste of Lincoln.

Beyond its culinary delights, Lincoln hosts an array of entertainment venues that cater to various interests. The downtown area is a hub of cultural activities, where theaters and concert halls present live performances, including plays, musicals, and concerts featuring both local and international talent.

Sports enthusiasts will find plenty to cheer for in Lincoln, as it is home to the University of

Nebraska's Cornhuskers. The city's passion for college sports creates an electrifying atmosphere during game days.

For a dose of history and art, visitors can explore museums and galleries showcasing the region's heritage and contemporary works. The Sheldon Museum of Art and the International Quilt Museum are must-visit places for art aficionados.

Nature lovers can escape to the city's scenic parks and gardens, perfect for leisurely strolls or picnics. Antelope Park and Sunken Gardens, with their vibrant blooms and tranquil landscapes, offer a refreshing break from urban life.

Whether you're seeking a memorable dining experience or an evening of entertainment,

Lincoln has something to captivate every individual. Its warm hospitality, coupled with the fusion of culinary delights and cultural offerings, make it a truly charming destination.

4.5 SPECIAL EVENTS IN LINCOLN

Lincoln plays host to a diverse range of exciting and memorable occasions that showcase the city's rich cultural heritage and community spirit.

One of the most eagerly anticipated events is the Lincoln Arts Festival, where talented artists from across the region converge to display their masterpieces. This extravaganza celebrates creativity, featuring live performances, interactive exhibits, and art workshops for all ages.

Sports enthusiasts gather in Lincoln each year for the thrilling Cornhusker Games, a multi-sport event that encourages active lifestyles and friendly competition. Participants of all skill levels can take part in various sports, fostering a sense of camaraderie and healthy living.

Lincoln's culinary scene comes alive during the Taste of Lincoln festival, a culinary extravaganza that brings together local chefs, food vendors, and restaurants. Attendees can savor delicious dishes while enjoying live music and family-friendly entertainment.

In the heart of summer, the Lincoln Balloon Festival paints the sky with a breathtaking display of hot air balloons, creating a mesmerizing sight for all to behold. The event offers tethered balloon rides and mesmerizing nighttime glow shows that leave visitors in awe.

The annual Star City Parade is a beloved tradition that unites the community with a vibrant procession of floats, marching bands, and dance troupes. This lively parade celebrates Lincoln's history, culture, and people, fostering a strong sense of unity and pride.

During the holiday season, the Lincoln Holiday Lights Festival transforms the city into a winter wonderland adorned with captivating light displays and festive decorations. Families come together to enjoy ice-skating, carriage rides, and visits with Santa Claus.

The Lied Center for Performing Arts hosts a series of Broadway shows, concerts, and theatrical performances, attracting both local talent and world-renowned artists. This cultural hub enriches the city's arts scene, making it a must-visit destination for art lovers.

Every year, the Lincoln Children's Zoo organizes a Boo at the Zoo event during Halloween, offering a safe and fun environment for kids to trick-or-treat and interact with friendly animals.

For those with a penchant for classic cars, the Annual Lincoln Car Show brings vintage automobiles to the forefront, allowing enthusiasts to marvel at stunning relics from the past.

Lincoln also takes immense pride in its annual Native American Powwow, an event that honors and celebrates the indigenous cultures that have shaped the region's history and identity.

With such an extensive lineup of special events throughout the year, Lincoln continues to captivate the hearts of all who visit, showcasing its welcoming community and vibrant spirit. No matter the time of year, there's always something extraordinary to experience in the capital of Nebraska.

CHAPTER 5: WESTERN NEBRASKA WONDERS

5.1 THE PANHANDLE REGION

The Panhandle Region in western Nebraska is a captivating and diverse landscape that has a unique blend of natural beauty and rich history. Stretching across the northwestern part of the state, it is characterized by its vast prairies, rolling hills, and rugged buttes, forming an awe-inspiring panorama that captures the hearts of all who visit.

Home to iconic landmarks such as Scotts Bluff National Monument and Chimney Rock, the Panhandle Region holds significant historical importance as a prominent route along the

Oregon Trail during the westward expansion of the United States. Travelers can immerse themselves in the footsteps of pioneers and explorers, imagining the challenges they faced in their pursuit of a better life.

The region's distinct climate, with hot summers and cold winters, supports a range of flora and fauna, making it a haven for nature enthusiasts. It offers numerous opportunities for outdoor adventures, including hiking, camping, and birdwatching, as well as excellent fishing in the nearby rivers and lakes.

In addition to its natural splendor, the Panhandle Region is proud of its vibrant communities and welcoming locals. From rodeos and county fairs to cultural events celebrating the heritage of the Native American tribes that once thrived in the area, there is always something fascinating to explore.

The agricultural industry plays a significant role in the region's economy, with vast stretches of farmland producing crops such as corn, wheat, and sorghum, contributing to the state's reputation as the "Cornhusker State."

In conclusion, the Panhandle Region of western Nebraska stands as a hidden gem, inviting visitors to experience the beauty of its landscapes, delve into the pages of history, and embrace the warmth of its communities. It remains a testament to the pioneering spirit that shaped the nation, and a place where nature and human heritage coexist in harmony.

5.2 SCOTTSBLUFF AND GERING

Located in western Nebraska, Scottsbluff and Gering are two charming communities that offer a captivating blend of natural beauty, rich history, and friendly hospitality. Nestled in the shadows of the iconic Scotts Bluff National Monument, the region is characterized by its striking landscapes and unique geological formations.

Scotts Bluff National Monument, a prominent landmark along the historic Oregon Trail, attracts visitors from far and wide with its towering cliffs and sweeping vistas. Hiking trails lead adventurers to breathtaking overlooks, where they can soak in panoramic views of the Platte River Valley and the surrounding plains.

Both Scottsbluff and Gering boast a strong sense of community, evident in their bustling downtown areas lined with local shops, restaurants, and cultural attractions. The legacy of the Oregon Trail is preserved in various museums and historical sites, providing insight into the area's past as a vital pioneer route.

The North Platte River meanders through the region, offering opportunities for outdoor enthusiasts to enjoy activities like fishing, kayaking, and picnicking along its scenic banks. The Wildcat Hills State Recreation Area, with its diverse wildlife and striking rock formations, presents further opportunities for exploration and appreciation of the region's natural wonders.

Throughout the year, the communities host numerous events and festivals that celebrate their heritage, arts, and local flavors. From farmers' markets showcasing fresh produce to music concerts that enliven the streets, there's always something to engage both residents and visitors.

Scottsbluff and Gering are not just inviting places for tourists but also provide a warm and welcoming environment for those who choose to call them home. The strong community spirit, coupled with the area's stunning landscapes, creates a special charm that leaves a lasting impression on all who venture to this western corner of Nebraska.

Whether it's relishing the awe-inspiring views from atop Scotts Bluff, delving into the region's pioneer past, or simply savoring the small-town ambiance, this dynamic duo of towns offers an unforgettable experience in the heart of the Great Plains.

5.3   CHIMNEY   ROCK   NATIONAL HISTORIC SITE

Chimney Rock National Historic Site, located in western Nebraska, is an awe-inspiring testament to the natural beauty and historical significance of the American West. Rising 325 feet above the surrounding plains, this iconic geological formation has captured the imaginations of travelers and explorers for centuries.

With its distinctive chimney-like appearance, the rock served as a prominent landmark for Native American tribes, fur traders, and pioneers journeying along the Oregon, California, and Mormon Trails during the 19th century. It was a beacon of hope and a symbol of progress, signifying the vast opportunities and challenges that lay ahead for those seeking a better life in the West.

Today, Chimney Rock remains a cherished symbol of the pioneering spirit, attracting visitors from across the globe to marvel at its unique geological structure and rich historical significance. The visitor center offers an immersive experience, providing insights into the lives of the brave souls who traversed these lands in search of new horizons.

As one stands at the base of Chimney Rock, surrounded by the vast expanse of the Great Plains, it is impossible not to feel a profound sense of reverence for the resilience and determination of those who came before. The panoramic views from the summit are breathtaking, offering a glimpse into the untamed beauty that once captivated the hearts of explorers and settlers alike.

The National Historic Site also includes well-maintained hiking trails, allowing visitors to explore the surrounding landscape and immerse themselves in the history of the region. Educational exhibits, interactive displays, and guided tours provide a deeper understanding of the cultural and geological significance of this natural wonder.

In addition to its historical and geological importance, Chimney Rock National Historic Site also serves as a sanctuary for various plant and animal species, contributing to the conservation efforts in the region.

Whether one seeks to connect with the spirit of the pioneers or simply revel in the stunning vistas of the American heartland, Chimney Rock National Historic Site offers a profound and unforgettable experience. It stands as a reminder of the enduring human spirit and the ever-changing landscapes that have shaped the course of American history.

5.4 SCOTTS BLUFF NATIONAL MONUMENT

Scotts Bluff National Monument, located in western Nebraska, stands as a magnificent testament to both the geological and historical significance of the American West. Rising dramatically from the plains, the monument is a prominent landmark that has guided travelers for centuries.

This iconic rock formation, composed of ancient volcanic ash and sedimentary rock, offers a captivating insight into the region's geological history. Erosion has shaped the bluffs over millennia, creating stunning ridges, spires, and buttes that command awe and admiration.

Beyond its geological marvels, Scotts Bluff is steeped in rich human history. For Native American tribes, it held spiritual and cultural significance, evident through numerous artifacts and petroglyphs found in the area. During the westward expansion of the 19th century, the Oregon Trail pioneers passed through here, leaving behind a legacy of their arduous journey.

Visitors to the monument can explore a network of trails that lead to breathtaking overlooks, offering panoramic views of the surrounding landscape. The visitor center houses informative exhibits, showcasing the stories of those who traversed the Oregon Trail and the challenges they faced.

Throughout the year, Scotts Bluff National Monument hosts various educational programs and events, providing a deeper understanding of the area's heritage and natural wonders. From wildflower blooms in the spring to vibrant foliage in the fall, each season brings its own unique charm to this iconic destination.

For nature enthusiasts, the monument's diverse flora and fauna offer plenty of opportunities for wildlife watching and bird spotting. Moreover, stargazers are in for a treat as the monument's remote location ensures minimal light pollution, making it an ideal spot for stargazing and night photography.

In summary, Scotts Bluff National Monument stands as a captivating fusion of geological wonder and human history. Its preservation allows modern-day explorers to connect with the past, appreciate the grandeur of nature, and marvel at the enduring spirit of those who ventured westward in pursuit of a new horizon.

5.5 WILDCAT HILLS STATE RECREATION AREA

The Wildcat Hills State Recreation Area stands as a true gem of natural beauty and outdoor adventure. With its rugged terrain and sweeping vistas, this enchanting area offers visitors a delightful escape from the hustle and bustle of everyday life.

The centerpiece of the park is the iconic Wildcat Hills, a series of majestic sandstone formations that have been shaped by millions of years of geological processes. These impressive hills serve as a haven for hikers, rock climbers, and nature enthusiasts eager to explore the area's unique flora and fauna.

Trails crisscross the park, leading visitors through diverse habitats, from ponderosa pine forests to open prairies, providing opportunities for wildlife spotting and birdwatching. As the sun sets, the skies come alive with a breathtaking display of stars, making it a perfect spot for stargazers and astrophotographers.

For those seeking a more immersive experience, camping facilities are available, allowing visitors to embrace the tranquility of the area. Campfires under the vast Nebraska sky create a sense of camaraderie and relaxation, providing the ideal setting for storytelling and forging lasting memories.

History enthusiasts will find intrigue in the remnants of pioneer and Native American settlements scattered throughout the region. These echoes of the past offer a glimpse into the rich cultural heritage that shaped the area.

Whether it's a day trip or an extended stay, Wildcat Hills State Recreation Area promises an unforgettable experience for all who venture into its rugged embrace. With its blend of scenic beauty, recreational activities, and historical significance, it stands as a testament to the enduring allure of Nebraska's western wilderness.

5.6 WESTERN NEBRASKA'S UNIQUE CULTURE

Western Nebraska has a captivating and distinct culture that sets it apart from other regions in the United States. Nestled between the vast prairies and the towering Rocky Mountains, this rugged landscape has shaped the lifestyle and traditions of its inhabitants for generations.

The region's rich Native American heritage, particularly that of the Lakota Sioux and the Cheyenne tribes, continues to influence its culture. Traditional ceremonies, art, and storytelling keep the spirit of their ancestors alive and infuse the local communities with a deep sense of history and pride.

Ranching has been a cornerstone of Western Nebraska's economy and culture for centuries. Cowboys, with their iconic hats and boots, still roam the vast grasslands, preserving a time-honored way of life. Rodeos and cattle drives remain popular events that celebrate the grit and resilience of these rugged individuals.

The pioneer spirit runs deep in the hearts of Western Nebraskans, as they celebrate their pioneering history with festivals and events that showcase the struggles and triumphs of those who settled the land. Visitors are welcomed with warm hospitality and a genuine openness to share their stories.

The unique fusion of Native American, cowboy, and pioneer influences is reflected in the region's arts and crafts. Intricate beadwork, leatherwork, and pottery showcase the talent and creativity of local artisans, and visitors can explore numerous galleries and craft shops.

Agriculture is also vital to Western Nebraska's culture, with fields of corn, wheat, and sunflowers stretching across the horizon. The agrarian lifestyle connects communities and fosters a strong sense of self-reliance and cooperation.

The wide-open spaces and breathtaking vistas have inspired generations of artists and writers, leading to a vibrant arts scene that flourishes in the region. Museums, art centers, and cultural events offer a glimpse into the soul of Western Nebraska.

Family values and community bonds are highly cherished, with close-knit towns and villages fostering a strong sense of belonging. Annual fairs, parades, and communal gatherings further strengthen these bonds, bringing people together to celebrate their shared heritage.

Western Nebraska's unique culture also embraces the joy of outdoor activities. Residents and visitors alike relish hiking, camping, fishing, and exploring the natural wonders of the area, such as Scotts Bluff National Monument and the Oregon Trail.

In this extraordinary corner of America, time seems to move at a different pace, and the values of the past blend harmoniously with the opportunities of the present. Western Nebraska's unique culture exudes a sense of authenticity and reverence for its roots, making it a captivating and enriching destination for all who wish to experience its charms.

CHAPTER 6: THE GREAT PLAINS AND SANDHILLS

6.1 OVERVIEW OF THE GREAT PLAINS

The Great Plains constitute a vast and iconic region in the heart of the United States. Stretching across the state, this geographical wonderland is characterized by its sweeping landscapes, rolling prairies, and immense natural beauty. Covering thousands of square miles, the Great Plains in Nebraska are a prime example of the quintessential American heartland.

The region boasts a diverse array of flora and fauna, from golden fields of wheat and corn to abundant grasslands teeming with wildlife. Home to a variety of native species like bison, pronghorn, and prairie dogs, the Great Plains offer a unique opportunity to witness nature in its unspoiled glory.

Besides its natural wonders, the Great Plains hold significant historical and cultural importance. It served as the hunting grounds and traditional territory of various Native American tribes long before European settlers arrived. The Oregon Trail and other historic routes crisscross the landscape, highlighting the area's pivotal role in the westward expansion of the United States.

Agriculture plays a central role in Nebraska's Great Plains, with vast farmlands and ranches dotting the countryside. The region's fertile soil and favorable climate have made it a leading producer of crops like corn, soybeans, and wheat, contributing significantly to the nation's food production.

Visitors to the Great Plains can immerse themselves in its unique charm, enjoying activities such as hiking, birdwatching, and stargazing. The wide-open spaces and tranquil vistas offer a chance for contemplation and a welcome escape from the bustle of urban life.

In conclusion, the Great Plains of Nebraska embody the spirit of America's heartland, showcasing the beauty of the natural world and the resilience of those who have called this region home for generations. From its rich history to its thriving agricultural landscape, the Great Plains offer an unforgettable experience that captures the essence of the American frontier.

6.2 SANDHILLS REGION

The Sandhills Region in Nebraska is a captivating and unique landscape that stretches across central and western parts of the state. Spanning over 19,300 square miles, it is one of the largest sand dune formations in the world. Comprising a mixture of grass-covered dunes and wetland valleys, the Sandhills create a stunning visual contrast with their undulating, wave-like patterns.

The region is renowned for its striking natural beauty, showcasing a diverse array of flora and fauna. The vast grasslands are home to a rich variety of wildlife, including pronghorn antelope, mule deer, coyotes, and numerous bird species. This makes it a paradise for nature enthusiasts and photographers, offering ample opportunities for wildlife observation and photography.

One of the most remarkable features of the Sandhills is the Ogallala Aquifer, a vast underground reservoir that provides water to the region's residents, livestock, and agricultural activities. The dunes act as a natural filter, purifying the water and making it a crucial resource for both the environment and human consumption.

Despite its arid appearance, the Sandhills Region is a treasure trove of hidden lakes, wetlands, and marshes, which serve as vital breeding grounds for migratory birds. These water bodies provide a welcome oasis amid the sand, attracting numerous waterfowl species during their annual journeys.

The Sandhills' beauty is not limited to its natural elements; it also holds a rich cultural heritage. Indigenous tribes have called this region home for centuries, leaving behind a legacy of history and traditions that continue to influence the area's identity.

The Sandhills Region is an ideal destination for ecotourism, where visitors can experience the serenity and solitude of the prairie landscape. Outdoor activities like hiking, birdwatching, and stargazing are popular among those seeking a close connection with nature.

As a sustainable and resilient ecosystem, the Sandhills continue to thrive, serving as a living testament to the power of preservation and conservation efforts. Its scenic vistas, unique geology, and abundant wildlife make it a true gem in the heart of Nebraska, welcoming all who venture to explore its natural wonders.

6.3 WILDLIFE AND NATURE RESERVES

The Great Plains and Sandhills of Nebraska encompass some of the most diverse and enchanting wildlife and nature reserves in the United States. Stretching across vast landscapes of rolling grasslands, prairies, and sand dunes, these regions offer a haven for an incredible array of flora and fauna.

In these expansive reserves, visitors have the opportunity to witness the iconic American bison roaming freely, along with pronghorn antelopes gracefully bounding across the plains. The area is also home to numerous bird species, from majestic bald eagles to colorful meadowlarks, making it a bird watcher's paradise.

One of the primary attractions is the Nebraska National Forest, which might surprise some as it's the largest human-planted forest in the entire United States. This forest stands as a testament to conservation efforts to restore the landscape and promote biodiversity. Furthermore, the Niobrara National Scenic River, meandering through these regions, adds to the allure, offering kayaking and canoeing opportunities, surrounded by stunning riverine scenery.

The Sandhills region, with its unique dune formations covered in prairie grasses, supports a delicate ecosystem that houses a variety of plant and animal species. It serves as a critical habitat for numerous migratory birds, creating vital nesting grounds.

In addition to the ecological significance, the Great Plains and Sandhills reserves provide a splendid chance for visitors to immerse themselves in the natural beauty of wide-open spaces and marvel at the stunning sunsets that stretch as far as the eye can see.

Conservation efforts in these areas have been commendable, with various organizations working to protect the delicate balance of the ecosystem, ensuring that future generations can cherish the splendor of the wildlife and nature reserves in the heart of Nebraska's Great Plains and Sandhills. Whether it's exploring the trails, camping under the stars, or simply soaking in the tranquility of these unspoiled landscapes, a visit to these reserves is a must for any nature enthusiast or those seeking to connect with the untamed spirit of the American wilderness.

CHAPTER 7: EASTERN NEBRASKA GEMS

7.1 THE MISSOURI RIVER VALLEY

The Missouri River Valley in eastern Nebraska is a region that encapsulates the state's natural beauty and historical significance. Carved by the mighty Missouri River over thousands of years, this valley boasts stunning landscapes, fertile plains, and a rich tapestry of flora and fauna.

The valley's rolling hills and lush greenery offer a picturesque view, attracting nature enthusiasts and photographers alike. The river's presence weaves its way into the heart of the valley, providing ample opportunities for boating, fishing, and water-based recreational activities.

The fertile soils of the Missouri River Valley have played a crucial role in the agricultural heritage of Nebraska. Its bountiful farmlands are dotted with cornfields, soybean crops, and picturesque farmsteads, showcasing the region's agricultural prowess.

Steeped in history, the Missouri River Valley holds a special place in the westward expansion of the United States. It served as a vital route for pioneers and explorers during the 19th century, leaving behind a legacy of old trading posts, historical landmarks, and museums that recount tales of the Oregon Trail and the Lewis and Clark Expedition.

Today, the valley is home to charming towns and cities that preserve their unique history while embracing modern development. Residents and visitors can indulge in the area's vibrant culture, experiencing local festivals, art exhibits, and delicious farm-to-table cuisine.

The Missouri River itself is a hub of activity, with riverboat cruises offering a chance to explore the waterway and take in the panoramic views of the surrounding landscape. Birdwatching enthusiasts will be delighted by the diverse avian species that inhabit the riverbanks, making it a bird watcher's paradise.

In addition to its natural splendor, the valley also presents opportunities for outdoor recreation, such as hiking, biking, and camping in the numerous state parks and recreation areas that dot the region.

The Missouri River Valley in eastern Nebraska is a captivating blend of nature's wonders and human history. Whether you seek adventure, tranquility, or a glimpse into the past, this region promises an unforgettable experience for all who venture into its embrace.

7.2 HISTORIC SITES IN EASTERN NEBRASKA

Eastern Nebraska is a region rich in history, and dotted with numerous fascinating historic sites that offer a glimpse into the area's past. From Native American heritage to pioneers' struggles, there's much to explore. Here are some of the notable historic sites in Eastern Nebraska:

Fort Atkinson State Historical Park: Located near Fort Calhoun, this reconstructed military outpost was the first United States Army post west of the Missouri River. Visitors can witness reenactments, explore the reconstructed buildings, and learn about the hardships faced by soldiers in the early 19th century.

Joslyn Castle: Situated in Omaha, this 35-room mansion is a prime example of Scottish Baronial architecture. Built in the late 19th century by wealthy businessman George Joslyn, the castle showcases opulent furnishings and stunning landscapes.

Lewis and Clark Landing: Located along the Omaha riverfront, this site commemorates the historic expedition of Lewis and Clark. It features interactive exhibits and sculptures, providing insight into the journey that opened up the West.

General Crook House Museum: Found in Omaha, this Victorian-era mansion once served as the residence of General George Crook, a prominent figure in the Indian Wars. The museum offers exhibits on Crook's military career and life in the late 1800s.

Arbor Lodge State Historical Park: In Nebraska City, this site was once the residence of J. Sterling Morton, the founder of Arbor Day. The beautiful mansion and its surrounding grounds are a testament to Morton's dedication to conservation and tree planting.

Museum of Nebraska Art (MONA): Located in Kearney, MONA showcases a vast collection of Nebraska-related art, preserving the state's artistic heritage.

Homestead National Monument of America: Located near Beatrice, this historic site commemorates the Homestead Act of 1862, which encouraged westward migration and settlement. Visitors can explore the original homestead claim and learn about the lives of early pioneers.

Chief Standing Bear Trail: This trail follows the route taken by Chief Standing Bear in 1879 as he fought for the recognition of Native Americans as "persons" under the law. The trail runs through numerous historic sites significant to Native American history in the region.

Willa Cather's Childhood Home: Found in Red Cloud, this historic site was the childhood home of renowned author Willa Cather. It inspired much of her literary work, and visitors can learn about her life and the influences that shaped her writing.

Stuhr Museum of the Prairie Pioneer: Located in Grand Island, this living history museum portrays pioneer life on the Nebraska prairie. It includes historic buildings, reenactments, and exhibits representing the challenges faced by early settlers.

These historic sites in Eastern Nebraska provide a captivating journey through time, offering visitors a chance to connect with the region's diverse past and the individuals who played a significant role in shaping its history.

7.3 LEWIS AND CLARK INTERPRETIVE CENTERS

The Lewis and Clark Interpretive Centers in eastern Nebraska offer captivating insights into the legendary journey of the Corps of Discovery led by Meriwether Lewis and William Clark. Located amid the scenic landscapes of the region, these centers serve as gateways to the past, immersing visitors in the epic expedition that shaped the nation's history.

Through meticulously curated exhibits, interactive displays, and multimedia presentations, visitors can relive the arduous and transformative exploration undertaken by Lewis and Clark from 1804 to 1806. The centers present a comprehensive narrative of the expedition's challenges, triumphs, encounters with indigenous tribes, and their impact on the western frontier.

As visitors step back in time, they learn about the Corps' encounters with the diverse flora and fauna of the area, the strategies they employed for navigation, and the cultural exchanges that took place along their journey. Life-sized replicas of boats and equipment used during the expedition further enhance the immersive experience.

The centers also pay tribute to the Native American tribes whose ancestral lands were traversed by Lewis and Clark. Special attention is given to the cultural heritage and wisdom of these indigenous communities, fostering a deeper understanding of their historical connection to the land.

Educational programs and guided tours cater to visitors of all ages, making it an ideal destination for families, students, and history enthusiasts alike. The centers' scenic locations, often situated near the original trail routes, offer a chance to explore the nearby natural beauty and appreciate the enduring legacy of the Lewis and Clark expedition in eastern Nebraska.

7.4 SMALL TOWN CHARMS

Located amid the picturesque landscape of eastern Nebraska. small town charms await to enchant visitors and residents alike. These quaint, close-knit communities exude a timeless appeal that harks back to simpler times and showcases the heartwarming essence of rural America.

The allure of these towns lies in their welcoming atmosphere and friendly locals, who are quick to offer warm greetings and lend a helping hand. Strolling down the main streets, lined with historic buildings and unique boutiques, creates a nostalgic ambiance that transports visitors to bygone eras.

Eastern Nebraska's small towns boast a rich cultural heritage, evident in their local festivals, art galleries, and museums, which celebrate the region's history and artistry. Every corner seems to hold a story, and the townspeople take great pride in sharing their tales.

As the seasons change, so does the charm of these towns. In the spring, blossoms paint the landscape with vibrant colors, and farmers' markets offer a taste of fresh produce. Summers are filled with outdoor concerts, fairs, and recreational activities that bring the community together.

Fall brings a breathtaking display of foliage, turning the landscape into a canvas of reds, oranges, and yellows. And when winter arrives, the towns are transformed into idyllic winter wonderlands, with cozy cafes, holiday lights, and cheerful festivities.

Beyond the aesthetics, the genuine hospitality of eastern Nebraska's small towns is what truly captivates visitors. Whether it's striking up a conversation with a local at the diner or participating in a community event, the sense of belonging is palpable.

For those seeking refuge from the fast-paced world, eastern Nebraska's small town charms offer a haven of tranquility, where time seems to slow down, and the genuine connections with people and nature reign supreme. It's a place where strangers are welcomed as friends, and the simple pleasures of life are cherished and celebrated.

7.5 WINERIES AND VINEYARDS

Eastern Nebraska is a burgeoning region for wineries and vineyards, boasting a unique and favorable climate that nurtures the growth of exquisite grapes. Situated in the heartland of the United States, this hidden gem has been steadily gaining recognition for its burgeoning wine industry.

The fertile soils, coupled with the region's warm summers and moderate winters, create an ideal environment for grape cultivation. Vintners in Eastern Nebraska have capitalized on this advantage, cultivating a diverse range of grape varieties, including Vitis vinifera and cold-hardy hybrids.

The scenic landscapes of rolling hills and picturesque rivers offer an enchanting backdrop for vineyard tours and wine tastings. Many wineries in the area have charming tasting rooms, where visitors can sample a wide array of wines, from smooth reds to crisp whites and delightful rosés.

The local winemakers take pride in their craft, focusing on sustainable and innovative techniques to produce high-quality wines that reflect the region's distinct terroir. The hospitality of the winery owners and staff adds to the overall experience, making visitors feel welcome and appreciated.

Eastern Nebraska's wine events and festivals are not to be missed. These gatherings provide an opportunity for both locals and tourists to celebrate the region's winemaking heritage, enjoy live music, savor delicious food pairings, and, of course, indulge in the finest wines the area has to offer.

With each passing year, the reputation of Eastern Nebraska's wineries and vineyards continues to grow, attracting wine enthusiasts from far and wide. Whether you are a seasoned oenophile or a curious novice, a visit to this burgeoning wine region promises an unforgettable and delightful experience for all.

CHAPTER 8: OUTDOOR ADVENTURES

8.1 HIKING AND NATURE TRAILS

Exploring Nebraska's natural beauty on foot is an unforgettable experience that connects visitors with its diverse ecosystems and rich wildlife.

The rugged and picturesque trails in Nebraska showcase the unique charm of the region, with opportunities to encounter fascinating flora and fauna along the way. Whether it's the lush woodlands of the Niobrara River Valley or the awe-inspiring panoramas from the Scotts Bluff National Monument, hikers will find themselves immersed in the wonders of nature.

One such highlight is the Indian Cave State Park, which boasts an extensive network of trails winding through limestone caves, hardwood forests, and scenic overlooks. For those seeking a more challenging hike, the rugged terrain of the Pine Ridge region presents opportunities for thrilling adventures.

Nebraska's diverse landscape caters to hikers of all levels, from leisurely strolls in the prairie grasslands to more demanding treks in the Badlands of Toadstool Geologic Park. Wildlife enthusiasts will revel in the chance to spot bison, elk, pronghorn, and a variety of bird species while traversing these trails.

Hiking in Nebraska also provides a chance to learn about the state's history and culture. Trails like the Lewis and Clark National Historic Trail offer a glimpse into the past as they follow the footsteps of the famous explorers.

Whether you're seeking solitude in the wilderness or looking to connect with fellow nature lovers, hiking in Nebraska provides an escape from the hustle and bustle of everyday life. It's an opportunity to breathe in the fresh air, appreciate the beauty of the great outdoors, and create lasting memories amidst the tranquility of nature.

8.2 CANOEING AND KAYAKING

In the heart of the Great Plains, Nebraska provides a serene and diverse landscape for canoeing and kayaking enthusiasts. With its winding rivers, calm lakes, and lush wetlands, the state presents a perfect playground for paddlers of all levels.

The Platte River, a prominent waterway in Nebraska, attracts adventurers seeking a leisurely float amid picturesque scenery. Its gentle currents allow beginners to feel at ease while absorbing the beauty of the surrounding wildlife and prairie vistas.

For those seeking a more challenging experience, the Niobrara River in the northern part of the state beckons. With its swift waters and occasional rapids, kayakers and canoers can test their skills and embark on an exhilarating journey through scenic canyons and pine-studded bluffs.

Nebraska's numerous reservoirs, such as Lake McConaughy and Harlan County Lake, are excellent spots for recreational paddling. These vast bodies of water provide ample space for water sports enthusiasts to explore, fish, or simply relax in a tranquil setting.

For nature enthusiasts, the Nebraska Sandhills offer an unforgettable paddling experience through marshlands and reed-filled lakes teeming with birdlife and unique flora.

Safety is paramount, and paddlers are encouraged to check water levels and weather conditions before setting off on their adventure. Whether you're a novice or an experienced paddler, Nebraska's waterways promise an unforgettable and rejuvenating experience amidst the state's natural splendor.

8.3 FISHING HOTSPOTS

There is an array of fantastic fishing hotspots in Nebraska that lure anglers from far and wide. With its diverse waterways and abundant fish species, there's something for every fishing enthusiast to enjoy in the Cornhusker State.

One of the most renowned fishing destinations is Lake McConaughy, a massive reservoir on the North Platte River. Its crystal-clear waters are teeming with walleye, white bass, and catfish, providing an unforgettable angling experience. Additionally, the calm waters of Sherman Reservoir offer excellent opportunities for catching largemouth bass and crappie.

The Missouri River, running along Nebraska's eastern border, is a prime location for catfish, particularly the channel and blue varieties, which can grow to impressive sizes. The Platte River, winding its way across the state, is another popular spot, with ample supplies of carp, channel catfish, and flathead catfish.

For trout fishing, look no further than the Snake River Falls and the Calamus Reservoir, both known for their thriving trout populations. Anglers can also explore the Sandhills lakes, where largemouth bass, bluegill, and northern pike abound.

Nebraska's small lakes and ponds are ideal for family fishing trips, offering opportunities to reel in sunfish, crappie, and bass, ensuring an enjoyable experience for anglers of all ages.

It's essential to remember that fishing regulations may vary from one location to another, so checking the latest guidelines and acquiring the necessary permits is crucial before embarking on any fishing expedition in Nebraska. Whether you're a seasoned angler seeking trophy catches or a novice looking for a relaxing day by the water, Nebraska's fishing hotspots promise an adventure you won't soon forget.

8.4 CAMPING IN NEBRASKA

Embarking on a camping adventure in Nebraska is a unique experience for nature enthusiasts. Nestled in the heart of the Great Plains, this Midwestern gem surprises visitors with its diverse landscapes and outdoor opportunities.

Picture yourself pitching your tent beside the pristine waters of Lake McConaughy, Nebraska's largest reservoir. As the sun sets, the crimson hues paint the sky, setting the stage for a mesmerizing night under the stars. Alternatively, head to the Pine Ridge region, where dense forests and rugged canyons provide a haven for hikers and wildlife lovers alike. Don't forget your camera, as the vistas here are breathtaking.

Nebraska's state parks are a camper's dream, boasting well-maintained campgrounds and facilities. Chimney Rock, a national historic site, beckons adventurers with its towering limestone spire, evoking the spirit of pioneering days. Meanwhile, the Niobrara National Scenic River offers canoeing and kayaking opportunities amidst the tranquil beauty of the sandstone cliffs and rolling hills.

If you're a birdwatcher, don't miss the annual spring migration along the Platte River. Witness the awe-inspiring spectacle of millions of cranes gathering in the wetlands, creating a symphony of sounds and colors as they take flight.

Nighttime in Nebraska's wilderness is equally captivating. As the campfire crackles, you'll be serenaded by the gentle chorus of crickets and frogs, reminding you of the simplicity and beauty of nature.

Camping in Nebraska also means indulging in its hearty farm-to-table cuisine. Savor local delicacies like steak, corn on the cob, and homemade pies, connecting you to the region's agricultural roots.

Remember to pack wisely for your camping trip, as the weather can be unpredictable. But whatever the conditions, the warmth and friendliness of Nebraskans will make you feel right at home.

In conclusion, camping in Nebraska offers a perfect blend of untamed wilderness and Midwestern charm. It's an opportunity to reconnect with nature, discover hidden gems, and create lasting memories amidst the beauty of this often overlooked but truly captivating state.

8.5 BIRDWATCHING SANCTUARIES

Within this vast and magnificent state, birdwatching sanctuaries have emerged as vital conservation areas, providing safe havens for various bird species and offering unparalleled opportunities for visitors to observe these magnificent creatures in their natural habitats.

Among the prominent birdwatching sanctuaries in Nebraska, one can find the famous Rowe Sanctuary along the Platte River. This sanctuary serves as a critical stopover for countless migratory birds, including sandhill cranes and snow geese, during their awe-inspiring spring migration.

Another gem is Fontenelle Forest, a unique sanctuary that provides a haven for numerous woodland bird species amidst its lush forested areas and tranquil trails. Visitors can spot colorful warblers, woodpeckers, and owls, making it a popular spot for both seasoned birdwatchers and novices.

For those seeking a prairie bird watching experience, the Spring Creek Prairie Audubon Center offers an array of grassland birds, such as meadowlarks, bobolinks, and various raptor species. The center also focuses on educational programs to raise awareness about conservation efforts.

Nebraska's bird watching sanctuaries are not only about observing birds but also about fostering an understanding of the delicate ecosystems that sustain these winged wonders. By promoting responsible birdwatching practices, these sanctuaries play a crucial role in conserving Nebraska's rich biodiversity for generations to come.

Whether one is an avid birder or simply appreciates the serenity of nature, Nebraska's bird watching sanctuaries offer an enchanting experience that captures the essence of the state's natural beauty and avian wonders.

CHAPTER 9: NEBRASKA'S HIDDEN TREASURES

9.1 OFF-THE-BEATEN-PATH DESTINATIONS

Nebraska, known for its vast prairies and friendly communities, offers a surprising array of off-the-beaten-path destinations that are often overlooked by travelers. Here are some hidden gems waiting to be explored:

Toadstool Geologic Park: This surreal badlands landscape in the northwest of the state features unique rock formations, ancient fossils, and otherworldly beauty.

Smith Falls State Park: Home to Nebraska's tallest waterfall, this remote park in the Sandhills region offers stunning nature trails and peaceful camping spots.

Carhenge: A quirky replica of England's Stonehenge, this attraction in Alliance is made entirely of vintage cars, creating a fascinating roadside stop.

Ashfall Fossil Beds State Historical Park: Discover prehistoric treasures as you explore this site with well-preserved ancient rhinos, horses, and other creatures that lived here millions of years ago.

Fort Robinson State Park: Delve into Nebraska's Wild West history by visiting this former military outpost turned park, featuring historic buildings and beautiful landscapes.

Arbor Lodge State Historical Park: The former mansion of J. Sterling Morton, the founder of Arbor Day, offers beautiful gardens and a glimpse into Nebraska's agricultural heritage.

Indian Cave State Park: Tucked along the Missouri River, this park boasts limestone caves, hiking trails, and spectacular views of the surrounding countryside.

Brownville: A quaint riverside town with a rich arts scene, historic buildings, and picturesque views of the Missouri River.

Valentine National Wildlife Refuge: Immerse yourself in nature by exploring this vast refuge, which is a haven for various bird species and other wildlife.

Lake McConaughy: Nebraska's largest reservoir offers opportunities for fishing, boating, and water sports amid the stunning backdrop of the Sandhills.

Kregel Windmill Factory Museum: Located in Nebraska City, this unique museum showcases the history and craftsmanship of windmills, an essential part of the state's rural past.

Smith Falls: Enjoy a peaceful canoe trip down the Niobrara River and witness the beauty of Smith Falls, a captivating waterfall surrounded by lush vegetation.

Stuhr Museum of the Prairie Pioneer: Travel back in time at this living history museum in Grand Island, where you can experience life on the prairie as it was in the 19th century.

High Plains Homestead: An authentic homestead experience in the Sandhills, offering lodging in cozy cabins and a taste of the Old West.

Courthouse and Jail Rocks: These geological formations, used as landmarks by pioneers, provide a unique opportunity for hiking and learning about the region's history.

Nebraska's off-the-beaten-path destinations offer an unforgettable journey through diverse landscapes and a chance to connect with the state's rich history and natural wonders. Whether you're an outdoor enthusiast, history buff, or simply seeking unique experiences, these hidden gems are sure to leave lasting memories of your visit to the Cornhusker State

9.2 QUIRKY AND UNUSUAL ATTRACTIONS

In Nebraska, travelers can discover a delightful array of quirky and unusual attractions that are sure to capture your imagination.

Carhenge - A unique replica of England's Stonehenge, made entirely from vintage cars, is an awe-inspiring sight located in Alliance, Nebraska.

The World's Largest Ball of Twine - Cawker City might have a famous twine ball, but Nebraska boasts its own in Cushman, attracting curious travelers from all over.

Museum of Shadows - In Plattsmouth, explore a bizarre collection of haunted artifacts and eerie items that are bound to send shivers down your spine.

Smith Falls Waterfall - Hidden away in the Sandhills, this remote waterfall is the tallest in Nebraska and offers a surreal, almost mystical experience.

Petrified Wood Gallery - Ogallala houses an impressive display of petrified wood, fossils, and rare gemstones, showcasing the natural wonders of the past.

Toadstool Geologic Park - Wander through a surreal landscape of ancient rock formations and badlands, resembling something straight out of a sci-fi movie.

Harold Warp's Pioneer Village - Minden hosts an enormous collection of Americana, showcasing over 50,000 unique items from bygone eras.

The Great Platte River Road Archway Monument - A monument that spans Interstate 80, taking visitors on a journey through the historical events that shaped the region.

Ashfall Fossil Beds State Historical Park - Witness an ancient, prehistoric fossil bed where the remains of rhinos, camels, and other creatures were perfectly preserved by volcanic ash.

Car Art Reserve - In Custer County, you'll find a whimsical display of sculptures made from old cars and automotive parts.

The Museum of Fur Trade - Satiate your curiosity in Chadron with artifacts and exhibits from the early days of the fur trade, an essential part of Nebraska's history.

World's Largest Time Capsule - Seward is home to a mammoth-sized time capsule, buried in 1975, and not set to be opened until the year 2025.

The Claussen-Leahy Maverick Run - A quirky annual race in Omaha where participants dress in their wildest costumes, making it an amusing sight for both runners and spectators.

Spinning Bridge - The Bob Kerrey Pedestrian Bridge in Omaha allows visitors to cross state lines while offering a unique and spinning experience.

Frank House - Kearney's historical mansion has a mysterious secret passageway and riddles that visitors must solve to uncover its hidden treasures.

Nebraska's offbeat attractions are a testament to the state's diversity and a reminder that adventure and wonder can be found in the most unexpected places. Embrace the peculiar and embark on a journey like no other in this captivating Midwestern state.

9.3 LOCAL FESTIVALS AND EVENTS

Throughout the year, communities across the state of Nebraska come together to revel in a variety of festivities, showcasing their unique traditions and passions.

One of the most anticipated events is the Nebraska State Fair, held annually in late August. This iconic gathering draws people from all corners of the state, featuring livestock exhibitions, agricultural displays, thrilling rides, and a wide array of delicious local cuisine. It's a true testament to Nebraska's agricultural roots and tight-knit community spirit.

For the music enthusiasts, the Maha Music Festival in Omaha is a must-attend. Celebrated during the summer, this event brings together local and national artists for a weekend of live performances across various genres, creating an electric atmosphere that resonates with attendees of all ages.

History buffs find delight in the Old West Balloon Fest in Mitchell. This festival pays homage to the pioneer days, offering hot air balloon rides, reenactments of historical events, and an immersive experience into Nebraska's frontier past.

As autumn sets in, Oktoberfest celebrations take center stage, with cities like Lincoln and Grand Island hosting lively events featuring traditional German music, dance, and of course, delicious bratwurst and beer.

In the vibrant city of Kearney, the Sandhill Crane Migration is a natural spectacle that attracts birdwatchers and nature enthusiasts from across the nation. Each spring, millions of cranes converge on the Platte River, creating an awe-inspiring sight that captivates visitors.

For a taste of the artistic side of Nebraska, the Art in the Garden festival in Seward brings together local artisans and craftsmen, showcasing their creative works amidst beautiful botanical gardens, creating a perfect blend of nature and art.

Rodeos hold a special place in the hearts of Nebraskans, and events like the Buffalo Bill Rodeo in North Platte embody the rugged spirit of the Wild West. Featuring bull riding, barrel racing, and cowboy poetry, it's a chance to experience the frontier heritage in a modern-day setting.

Sports lovers revel in the college football season, with fervent support for the Nebraska Cornhuskers bringing the community together in a sea of red and white, creating an electrifying atmosphere that spreads far beyond the stadium.

No matter the season, Nebraska's local festivals and events offer a chance to experience the state's warmth, friendliness, and sense of community. Whether you're a resident or a visitor, these celebrations are an invitation to embrace the heart and soul of Nebraska.

9.4 HAUNTED PLACES AND GHOST STORIES

Nebraska holds a chilling allure with its haunted places and ghost stories. Among its eerie locales, the "Devil's Nest" stands out. This cliffside area near Dakota City is said to be haunted by the spirits of Native Americans who lost their lives in battles fought here long ago. Locals speak of eerie apparitions and strange sounds that emanate from the area at night.

Another spine-chilling site is the historic "Cotner College" in Lincoln. Abandoned for years, it is rumored to be haunted by the ghost of a former student who tragically passed away under mysterious circumstances. Visitors have reported hearing phantom footsteps echoing in empty hallways and doors slamming shut on their own.

The "Hummel Park" in Omaha has its own dark reputation. As night falls, a ghostly specter, known as the "Devil's Slide," is said to glide down the steep hillside. This eerie entity has spooked countless visitors and added to the park's haunted reputation.

In the quaint town of Brownville, the historic "Hotel Stephenson" is notorious for its ghostly guests. Guests have reported flickering lights, sudden drops in temperature, and strange shadows lurking in the hallways. Some even claim to have encountered the spirit of a former owner who refuses to leave.

Nebraska's old hospitals also have their share of ghostly tales. The "York Cold Storage Building" in York, formerly a hospital in the early 1900s, is rumored to be haunted by the souls of patients who met tragic ends. Visitors often experience unexplained feelings of dread and hear phantom whispers as they explore the decaying structure.

The "Jennie Edmundson Memorial Hospital" in Council Bluffs, just across the border in Iowa, is linked to a ghostly legend. Many believe that the spirit of Jennie Edmundson herself, a prominent benefactor, roams the halls and brings comfort to patients in times of need.

These are just a few of the haunted places and ghost stories that add a chilling dimension to the history of Nebraska. Whether you believe in the supernatural or not, the state's eerie legends and spectral encounters continue to captivate the imagination of locals and visitors alike, leaving a lingering sense of mystery and intrigue.

CHAPTER 10: CULINARY DELIGHTS

10.1 ICONIC NEBRASKA FOODS

Talking about culinary delights, Nebraska has a rich culinary heritage with a delightful array of iconic foods that reflect its agricultural abundance and cultural influences. From hearty farm-to-table dishes to sweet treats that evoke nostalgia, here are some of Nebraska's most iconic foods:

Runza: A beloved Nebraska comfort food, the Runza is a savory yeast bread pocket filled with seasoned ground beef, onions, and cabbage. Its roots trace back to German-Russian immigrants who settled in the state, making it a tasty symbol of Nebraska's heritage.

Bison Burger: With vast prairies that once hosted vast herds of bison, it's no surprise that the Bison Burger is an emblematic Nebraska dish. This lean and flavorful alternative to traditional beef burgers showcases the state's commitment to sustainable and locally sourced foods.

Corn on the Cob: As a leading producer of corn, Nebraskans relish fresh and tender corn on the cob during the summer months. Grilled, boiled, or slathered with butter, this classic crop is a quintessential taste of Nebraska's agricultural prowess.

Reuben Sandwich: Though its exact origins are debated, the Reuben Sandwich's popularity in Nebraska is undeniable. Layers of corned beef, sauerkraut, Swiss cheese, and Russian dressing nestled between rye bread make for a delectable treat.

Dorothy Lynch Dressing: This tangy, sweet, and creamy dressing is a Nebraska invention, and it has gained a loyal following both within the state and beyond. It adds a unique flair to salads, sandwiches, and various recipes.

Cherry Pie: In the state's Cherry County, aptly named for its abundant cherry trees, Cherry Pie stands out as a celebrated dessert. Made with tart Montmorency cherries, this pie is a perfect balance of sweet and sour.

Kool-Aid: Created by Edwin Perkins in Hastings, Nebraska, Kool-Aid has become a beloved symbol of childhood refreshment worldwide. Its powdery concoctions and vibrant flavors have delighted generations of Nebraskans.

Dorothy's Popcorn: Named after the iconic character Dorothy from "The Wizard of Oz," this popcorn is a Nebraska gourmet delight. Often coated in a sweet and buttery glaze, it's an irresistible snack during movie nights or any social gathering.

Steak: As a state renowned for its beef production, enjoying a mouthwatering Nebraska steak is a must. From succulent ribeyes to tender filet mignons, this state knows how to cook a mean steak.

Scotcheroos: A delectable dessert bar featuring a blend of peanut butter, butterscotch, and chocolate, Scotcheroos are a favorite at picnics, potlucks, and family gatherings all across Nebraska.

These iconic Nebraska foods not only satisfy the taste buds but also celebrate the state's history, culture, and natural bounty, making them an integral part of the Nebraska experience for locals and visitors alike.

10.2 CLASSIC STEAK HOUSES

Classic Steak Houses in Nebraska are a quintessential dining experience that celebrates the state's rich culinary heritage. Known for their warm hospitality and delectable offerings, these establishments have become iconic destinations for locals and visitors alike.

Nebraska's classic steak houses exude a timeless charm with their rustic decor, wooden accents, and cozy ambience. Patrons can expect to indulge in top-quality, locally sourced, and perfectly aged beef, cooked to perfection over open flames or on traditional grills. The steaks are often accompanied by an array of mouthwatering sides like loaded baked potatoes, creamed spinach, and crisp salads.

These establishments take immense pride in showcasing the state's agricultural prowess, emphasizing the farm-to-table philosophy. Their commitment to quality extends beyond the steak, with an impressive selection of Nebraska wines and craft beers that perfectly complement the flavors of the cuisine.

Stepping into one of these classic steak houses is like taking a nostalgic journey back in time, as they have stood the test of time, preserving the essence of Nebraska's culinary heritage. Whether it's a celebratory occasion or a casual dinner with loved ones, these establishments offer an unforgettable dining experience that leaves guests with lasting memories of hearty meals and Midwestern hospitality.

The friendly and attentive staff further enhance the dining experience, ensuring that patrons feel right at home from the moment they walk through the door. Moreover, many of these steak houses have become gathering spots for the community, fostering a sense of camaraderie among locals.

Nebraska's classic steak houses are not just places to eat; they are cultural landmarks that embody the state's traditions and values. They serve as a reminder of simpler times while adapting to modern culinary preferences, making them a timeless and cherished aspect of Nebraska's culinary landscape.

So, whether you're a devoted steak enthusiast or a curious food lover, exploring the classic steak houses of Nebraska promises an authentic and savory journey that captures the heart of the Midwest.

10.3 FARM-TO-TABLE EXPERIENCES

Nebraska's Farm-to-Table movement celebrates the essence of sustainable agriculture, where fresh, organic produce is sourced directly from local farms and delivered straight to the table. Visitors can revel in the rich flavors of sun-ripened tomatoes, crisp sweetcorn, succulent grass-fed beef, and an array of other farm-fresh delights.

The state's close-knit farming communities take immense pride in preserving their agricultural heritage, and this passion shines through in every dish served. From charming family-owned restaurants to vibrant farmers' markets, Nebraska offers diverse settings to savor the delectable creations crafted with utmost care and culinary expertise.

Tourists can indulge in guided farm tours, witnessing the farm-to-table journey firsthand, understanding the sustainable practices employed, and even engaging in activities like fruit picking or cheese-making. The warm hospitality of Nebraska's farmers adds a personal touch, making the experience even more memorable.

In addition to the gastronomic delights, Farm-to-Table experiences in Nebraska also offer a deeper connection to nature, allowing visitors to appreciate the hard work and dedication of those who cultivate the land. The experience fosters a profound appreciation for locally sourced ingredients and the impact of supporting local farmers and their communities.

Whether it's a simple yet heartwarming farm breakfast, a sophisticated dinner made from seasonal produce, or a delightful picnic amidst the picturesque countryside, Nebraska's Farm-to-Table experiences captivate the senses and leave an indelible mark on every food lover's heart. Immerse yourself in the flavors of the heartland, and you'll discover a culinary adventure that resonates with the soul.

10.4 CRAFT BREWERIES AND DISTILLERIES

In Nebraska, the thriving craft brewery and distillery scene has captivated both locals and visitors alike, offering a diverse range of handcrafted libations. From the charming streets of Omaha to the scenic countryside, these establishments have become vibrant hubs of creativity and community.

Craft breweries in Nebraska pride themselves on their unique and innovative brews, pushing the boundaries of traditional beer-making. With a focus on quality and flavor, they often incorporate locally sourced ingredients, paying homage to the state's agricultural heritage. Whether you're a fan of hoppy IPAs, smooth stouts, or crisp lagers, there's a craft brewery in Nebraska that can cater to your taste.

Similarly, Nebraska's distilleries have also gained recognition for their dedication to craftsmanship. They produce small-batch spirits, such as whiskey, vodka, gin, and rum, using time-honored techniques and a passion for perfection. Touring these distilleries gives visitors a chance to witness the intricate distillation process and learn about the art of aging spirits.

Many craft breweries and distilleries in Nebraska have transformed their spaces into inviting taprooms and tasting rooms, fostering a warm and welcoming atmosphere. It's common to find friendly brewers and distillers eager to share their knowledge and stories with enthusiasts and newcomers alike.

Nebraska's craft beverage scene isn't just about the drinks; it's about community too. These establishments often collaborate with local artisans, musicians, and food vendors, hosting events that celebrate the region's culture and creativity. Visitors can enjoy live music, art exhibitions, and delicious food pairings alongside their handcrafted beverages.

Beyond their local appeal, some of Nebraska's craft breweries and distilleries have garnered national recognition, winning prestigious awards for their exceptional products. This recognition has put Nebraska on the map as a destination for beer and spirits enthusiasts from around the country.

With the continued growth and innovation of craft breweries and distilleries in Nebraska, the state's beverage industry is set to thrive for years to come. As consumers increasingly appreciate the artistry and quality behind these handcrafted libations, the industry is likely to expand, attracting more talented brewers and distillers to the area.

Whether you're a seasoned craft beverage connoisseur or just beginning your exploration of the world of artisanal drinks, Nebraska's craft breweries and distilleries offer a delightful and unforgettable experience that highlights the best of what the state has to offer.

CHAPTER 11: FAMILY-FRIENDLY FUN

11.1 KID-FRIENDLY ATTRACTIONS

In Nebraska, visitors get thrilled by the variety of delightful and kid-friendly attractions that promise to create unforgettable family memories. Here are some of the top destinations:

Omaha's Henry Doorly Zoo and Aquarium: Renowned as one of the world's best zoos, it offers an immersive experience with fascinating exhibits like the Desert Dome and the Lied Jungle, where kids can get up close to exotic animals.

Lincoln Children's Zoo: Designed with young ones in mind, this zoo features interactive encounters, a splash pad, and a petting zoo, providing endless fun and educational opportunities.

Strategic Air Command & Aerospace Museum: Budding aviators will be thrilled by the extensive collection of aircraft and space artifacts, including flight simulators and hands-on exhibits.

Lee G. Simmons Wildlife Safari Park: Located near Ashland, this park allows kids to observe native North American wildlife in a natural environment from the comfort of a tram.

Fontenelle Forest Nature Center: A nature lover's paradise, offering hiking trails, treetop adventure courses, and interactive exhibits to explore the wonders of the great outdoors.

Stuhr Museum of the Prairie Pioneer: Step back in time and experience life on the prairie with historical reenactments, hands-on activities, and engaging exhibits.

Omaha Children's Museum: A haven for creativity and exploration, this museum boasts interactive displays, art workshops, and a science center sure to captivate young minds.

Pioneer Village: In Minden, this living history museum showcases artifacts from Nebraska's pioneering past, offering educational experiences and demonstrations.

Wildlife Safari State Recreation Area: Families can embark on a safari-style adventure while observing bison, elk, and other native species in their natural habitat.

Omaha's Fun-Plex Water Park & Rides: Beat the summer heat with thrilling water slides, wave pools, and amusement rides suitable for all ages.

From encounters with animals to historical adventures and nature exploration, Nebraska provides an exciting array of kid-friendly attractions that will leave families with cherished memories for years to come.

11.2 EDUCATIONAL AND INTERACTIVE MUSEUMS

Nebraska is home to a fascinating array of educational and interactive museums that cater to diverse interests and ages, making it a must-visit destination for history buffs, science enthusiasts, and curious minds of all kinds. These museums offer a captivating blend of interactive exhibits, hands-on activities, and engaging displays that make learning a thrilling experience.

The Strategic Air Command & Aerospace Museum in Ashland takes visitors on an immersive journey through aviation and aerospace history, featuring vintage aircraft and simulators that allow visitors to experience the thrill of flight firsthand.

For those interested in natural history, the University of Nebraska State Museum in Lincoln, also known as Morrill Hall, showcases an impressive collection of fossils and exhibits that shed light on the state's prehistoric past and its diverse ecosystems.

The Omaha Children's Museum is a haven for families with young children, offering a wide range of interactive exhibits that promote learning through play. From science experiments to art projects, kids are encouraged to explore and discover at their own pace.

The Durham Museum, housed in Omaha's Union Station, is a treasure trove of local history, displaying artifacts and interactive exhibits that recount the region's cultural heritage, from its railroad legacy to the pioneer era.

The Museum of American Speed in Lincoln is a paradise for automobile enthusiasts, featuring an extensive collection of vintage race cars and engines, along with hands-on displays that illustrate the evolution of automotive technology.

In addition to these prominent museums, Nebraska boasts several smaller but equally engaging institutions, such as the Museum of Nebraska Art in Kearney, which celebrates the state's artistic heritage, and the Great Platte River Road Archway Monument in Kearney, an interactive monument tracing the journey of pioneers along the Oregon Trail.

Whether you're traveling solo, with family, or in a school group, Nebraska's educational and interactive museums promise a delightful blend of entertainment and knowledge, offering visitors a chance to immerse themselves in the captivating realms of science, history, art, and technology.

11.3 OUTDOOR ACTIVITIES FOR FAMILIES

There are a lot of outdoor activities for families to enjoy together in Nebraska. From the wide open prairies to lush state parks, there's something for everyone to experience and create lasting memories. Here are some fantastic outdoor activities that families can partake in:

Hiking and Nature Walks: Nebraska boasts numerous scenic trails and nature walks suitable for all ages and fitness levels. Families can explore stunning vistas, encounter local wildlife, and discover the state's unique flora.

Camping: Spending a night under the starry skies is a wonderful way for families to bond.

Nebraska's well-maintained campgrounds provide a chance to escape the hustle and bustle of city life and enjoy quality time around a campfire.

Fishing: The state is dotted with lakes, rivers, and reservoirs that are perfect for fishing. Kids can learn to cast a line and perhaps catch their first fish, making it a memorable experience for the whole family.

Wildlife Viewing: Nebraska is home to an abundance of wildlife, including birds, deer, and bison. Families can participate in guided tours or explore wildlife areas on their own, keeping a lookout for fascinating creatures.

Canoeing and Kayaking: With several scenic waterways, families can paddle together, enjoying the serenity of the rivers and lakes while appreciating the natural beauty around them.

Geocaching: An excellent outdoor adventure for tech-savvy families, geocaching involves using GPS devices to find hidden treasures scattered across the state, adding a touch of excitement to exploration.

Picnicking: Nebraska's parks and recreational areas offer perfect spots for picnics. Families can relish delicious meals surrounded by nature's beauty, creating an idyllic setting for relaxation and fun.

Cycling: Biking trails, both on-road and off-road, allow families to pedal through charming landscapes and picturesque scenery, encouraging a healthy and enjoyable activity.

Hot Air Balloon Rides: For a unique and unforgettable experience, families can take hot air balloon rides, offering a bird's-eye view of Nebraska's enchanting landscapes.

Horseback Riding: Several ranches in Nebraska offer horseback riding opportunities, where families can ride through the plains and feel like true cowboys and cowgirls.

Berry and Fruit Picking: During the harvest season, families can visit orchards and berry farms to pick fresh produce together, creating cherished memories and enjoying delicious fruits.

Outdoor Movie Nights: Some parks host outdoor movie nights during the summer, where families can watch family-friendly films under the stars, adding a touch of magic to their evenings.

Stargazing: Away from the city lights, Nebraska's clear skies offer a spectacular stargazing experience. Families can identify constellations and marvel at the wonders of the universe.

Nature Centers and Museums: Numerous nature centers and museums throughout Nebraska provide interactive exhibits and programs, educating families about the region's unique ecosystems and history.

Sand Dune Exploration: In certain areas of the state, families can explore vast sand dunes, providing a unique and unexpected landscape to hike and play.

With such a wide array of outdoor activities to choose from, families visiting or residing in Nebraska can enjoy quality time together while immersing themselves in the state's natural wonders.

11.4 TIPS FOR TRAVELING WITH CHILDREN

Traveling with children to Nebraska can be a fun and rewarding experience for the whole family. To ensure a smooth and enjoyable trip, consider these essential tips:

Plan ahead: Research Nebraska's family-friendly attractions and activities in advance, and create a flexible itinerary that accommodates the interests and energy levels of your children.

Pack wisely: Bring essential items such as diapers, snacks, entertainment (books, toys, games), and comfortable clothing suitable for various weather conditions.

Safety first: Keep important documents, like passports and medical records, in a secure place. Also, carry a basic first-aid kit for any minor mishaps.

Choose child-friendly accommodations: Look for hotels or vacation rentals with amenities like play areas, pools, and cribs or rollaway beds.

Keep them engaged: Encourage your children to participate in planning the trip and engage them during the journey with interactive games or educational activities.

Plan frequent breaks: Kids need time to stretch their legs and burn off energy, so the schedule stops at parks or playgrounds along your route.

Try local cuisine: Introduce your children to Nebraska's regional dishes, but also have familiar snacks on hand for picky eaters.

Be weather-prepared: Check the weather forecast and dress appropriately to ensure your

191

children are comfortable during outdoor activities.

Explore nature: Nebraska boasts beautiful parks and natural wonders, providing an opportunity for your kids to connect with nature.

Visit interactive museums: Nebraska has several children's museums and science centers where kids can learn while having fun.

Involve them in local culture: Attend family-friendly events or festivals to experience the state's culture together.

Capture the memories: Encourage your children to keep a travel journal or take photos to remember the trip.

Embrace flexibility: Be prepared for detours and changes in plans – sometimes the best experiences happen spontaneously.

Plan for downtime: Include some downtime in your schedule, as traveling can be overwhelming for children.

Mind the pace: Avoid cramming too many activities in one day, as kids can tire easily.

Be patient: Traveling with children can be challenging at times, so practice patience and understanding.

Safety in transportation: Ensure your children are safely secured in car seats or seat belts during travel.

Teach them about the destination: Engage your children in learning about Nebraska's history, culture, and wildlife before the trip.

Respect local rules and customs: Teach your kids to be mindful of local customs and traditions.

Stay hydrated: Carry water bottles and encourage your children to drink regularly, especially in warmer weather.

Remember, the key to a successful trip is to strike a balance between planned activities and flexibility, so everyone can enjoy the journey and the destination. Happy travels to Nebraska with your children!

CHAPTER 12: PRACTICALITIES

12.1 SAFETY AND HEALTH TIPS

To ensure a smooth and problem free trip to Nebraska, it is imperative that travelers pay attention to the following tips:

Stay Hydrated: Nebraska's climate can be unpredictable, so it's essential to drink plenty of water, especially during hot summer days to avoid dehydration.

Sun Protection: Protect yourself from harmful UV rays by wearing sunscreen, sunglasses, and a wide-brimmed hat when spending time outdoors.

Tornado Preparedness: Nebraska is part of "Tornado Alley," so have a plan in place for severe weather. Identify a safe shelter and stay updated on weather alerts.

Road Safety: Observe speed limits, wear seat belts, and avoid distractions while driving to prevent accidents on the state's highways and rural roads.

Wildlife Awareness: When exploring Nebraska's natural beauty, be mindful of potential encounters with wildlife, including snakes and insects. Keep a safe distance and avoid provoking animals.

Water Safety: Whether swimming in lakes or rivers, always be cautious and aware of water currents, and never swim alone.

Food Safety: Follow proper food handling and storage guidelines to avoid foodborne illnesses, especially during picnics and outdoor events.

Stay Informed: Stay updated on health advisories, local news, and emergency information to make informed decisions in times of crisis.

Mental Health: Pay attention to your mental well-being and seek support when needed. Connect with local resources and support groups if you're facing challenges.

Fire Safety: If camping or using open fires, ensure you have a safe distance from vegetation and that the fire is entirely extinguished before leaving.

Workplace Safety: Employers and employees should adhere to safety regulations and protocols to prevent accidents and ensure a safe working environment.

Air Quality: During periods of poor air quality, especially in cities, limit outdoor activities, and consider wearing masks if you are sensitive to pollutants.

Allergies: Nebraska's vast landscapes can trigger allergies for some people, so be prepared with necessary medications and consult a doctor if needed.

Vaccinations: Stay up-to-date with vaccinations, including flu shots, to protect yourself and others from preventable diseases.

Exercise Caution in Outdoor Activities: Whether hiking, biking, or boating, be cautious and follow safety guidelines to minimize the risk of injuries.

Remember, safety and health are everyone's responsibility. By being aware and proactive, you can enjoy all that Nebraska has to offer while minimizing potential risks and staying well.

12.2 MONEY AND BANKING

As with many other states, the financial system in Nebraska is anchored by a network of banks and credit unions that serve both individuals and businesses.

In major cities like Omaha and Lincoln, one can find a plethora of national and regional banks catering to various financial needs. These institutions offer a wide array of services, including checking and savings accounts, loans, mortgages, and investment opportunities. Moreover, they play a crucial role in facilitating economic growth by extending credit to local businesses and entrepreneurs.

Nebraska's banking industry is subject to strict regulations and oversight, ensuring stability and consumer protection. The Nebraska Department of Banking and Finance diligently supervises financial institutions, safeguarding the interests of depositors and investors.

In addition to traditional banking, the state also embraces modern advancements in fintech.

Online banking, mobile payment platforms, and digital wallets are gaining popularity, providing convenient options for Nebraskans to manage their finances.

Furthermore, Nebraska's agricultural sector significantly impacts its economy. Agricultural banks are pivotal in supporting farmers with tailored financial solutions, helping them navigate through the challenges of the industry and promoting agricultural prosperity.

As the state continues to evolve, financial literacy and education play an essential role in empowering the residents to make informed decisions about money management. Various initiatives and programs aimed at promoting financial literacy have been implemented across the state.

In conclusion, money and banking in Nebraska form the backbone of the state's economy, fostering growth and prosperity. With a well-regulated banking system and a focus on innovation, Nebraskans are well-equipped to navigate the financial landscape, paving the way for a prosperous future.

12.3 TRAVELING RESPONSIBLY

When traveling to Nebraska, it is essential for visitors to embrace responsible travel practices that respect the environment, culture, and local communities. Here are some guidelines to ensure a positive impact during your trip:

Preserve Natural Beauty: Nebraska boasts stunning landscapes and diverse wildlife. Practice Leave No Trace principles by refraining from littering, staying on marked trails, and respecting wildlife habitats.

Support Local Economy: Opt to stay in locally-owned accommodations, dine at local eateries, and shop from small businesses to contribute directly to the state's economy.

Cultural Sensitivity: Embrace the rich history and traditions of Nebraska's indigenous communities by being respectful, seeking permission for photography, and learning about their customs.

Water Conservation: Given Nebraska's agricultural nature, conserve water wherever possible by minimizing usage and reporting any water waste.

Reduce, Reuse, Recycle: Make a conscious effort to reduce waste by carrying a reusable water bottle and shopping bag, and recycle whenever facilities are available.

Public Transportation and Carpooling: Whenever feasible, utilize public transportation or carpool to reduce carbon emissions and traffic congestion.

Energy Conservation: Conserve energy in your accommodations by turning off lights, air conditioning, and heating when not needed.

Wildlife Protection: Avoid disturbing or feeding wildlife, as this can alter their natural behaviors and cause harm.

Learn About Local Wildlife: Familiarize yourself with the native species of Nebraska, and consider supporting conservation efforts if possible.

Respect Private Property: Seek permission before entering private land or taking photographs on private property.

Engage in Responsible Photography: Be mindful of the impact of your photography, ensuring it does not disturb wildlife or local communities.

Support Conservation Organizations: Contribute to local conservation groups dedicated to preserving Nebraska's natural wonders.

Sustainable Fishing and Hunting: If you plan to fish or hunt during your visit, follow local regulations and guidelines to ensure sustainable practices.

Minimize Plastic Usage: Avoid single-use plastics and choose eco-friendly alternatives.

Educate Yourself: Learn about Nebraska's environmental challenges and efforts toward sustainability, and consider how you can play a part in supporting these initiatives.

By following these responsible travel practices, visitors can leave a positive footprint on Nebraska while enjoying all that this beautiful state has to offer.

12.4 APPS AND WEBSITE LINKS TO NEBRASKA MAPS AND OTHER INFORMATION

Here are some linked websites and apps that provide digital maps and crucial information like weather forecasts, traffic areas, and transportation in Nebraska:

Google Maps (Website and App)

Website: https://www.google.com/maps

Google Maps is one of the most popular and widely used mapping applications. It provides detailed maps, driving directions, real-time traffic updates, and public transportation information for cities and towns in Nebraska.

Waze (Website and App)

Website: https://www.waze.com

Waze is a community-based navigation app that offers real-time traffic information, road conditions, and alternative routes. It's particularly helpful for getting accurate traffic data in Nebraska's urban areas.

National Weather Service (NWS) - Omaha/Valley Office (Website)

Website: https://www.weather.gov/omaha

The NWS Omaha/Valley office provides official weather forecasts, warnings, and weather-related information for Nebraska. It's a reliable source to stay informed about weather conditions in the state.

The Weather Channel (Website and App)

Website: https://weather.com
The Weather Channel website and app offer up-to-date weather forecasts, radar maps, and severe weather alerts for cities across Nebraska.

Nebraska Department of Transportation (NDOT) (Website)

Website: https://dot.nebraska.gov
The NDOT website provides information on road conditions, construction updates, and traffic

incidents to help you plan your travels more effectively.

Moovit (App)

Website: https://moovitapp.com

Moovit is a public transit app that covers transportation options such as buses, trains, and light rails in Nebraska's major cities. It provides real-time schedules and trip planning.

Transit (App)

Website: https://transitapp.com

Transit is another app that helps you navigate public transportation in Nebraska. It offers real-time arrival information for buses and trains, as well as trip planning features.

AccuWeather (Website and App)

Website: https://www.accuweather.com
AccuWeather provides detailed weather forecasts, radar maps, and storm alerts for various locations in Nebraska.

Weather Underground (Website and App)

Website: https://www.wunderground.com
Weather Underground offers hyper-local weather forecasts, interactive radar maps, and severe weather alerts for cities in Nebraska.

By using these linked websites and apps, you'll have access to digital maps and crucial information to help you plan your routes, stay informed about weather conditions, and navigate transportation efficiently in Nebraska.

12.5 CREATING AN ITINERARY

Here is a recommended 7 day itinerary for a trip to Nebraska:

Nebraska, often referred to as the "Cornhusker State," is a destination with a wealth of natural beauty, history, and unique experiences waiting to be explored.

This itinerary is designed to give travelers a taste of the state's diverse landscapes, cultural heritage, and local charm.

Day 1: Arrival in Omaha

Arrive at Eppley Airfield in Omaha, Nebraska's largest city.

Check into a hotel and relax after your journey.

Explore the Old Market District, known for its historic buildings, boutique shops, and excellent dining options.

Enjoy a dinner at a local restaurant to sample some regional specialties.

Day 2: Omaha Attractions

Start the day at the Henry Doorly Zoo & Aquarium, one of the best zoos in the country, with exhibits showcasing diverse wildlife.

Visit the Joslyn Art Museum to appreciate a collection of both American and European art.

Stroll through the Lauritzen Gardens, a beautiful botanical garden.

In the evening, experience the vibrant nightlife and live music scene in the city.

Day 3: Lincoln and the State Capital

Travel to Lincoln, Nebraska's capital city, about an hour's drive from Omaha.

Explore the Nebraska State Capitol building, renowned for its unique architecture and beautiful interior.

Visit the University of Nebraska-Lincoln campus, taking a leisurely walk around its historic grounds.

Delve into the past at the Nebraska History Museum to learn about the state's rich heritage.

Enjoy a relaxing evening at a local park or join a sports event if it's in season.

Day 4: Kearney - Archway and Nature

Head west to Kearney, stopping at the Great Platte River Road Archway Monument to discover the history of the westward expansion.

Explore the Museum of Nebraska Art, displaying a vast collection of regional art.
Visit the Fort Kearny State Historical Park to learn about the Oregon Trail and the Pony Express.
Spend the night in Kearney.

Day 5: Sandhills and Scottsbluff

Journey through Nebraska's unique Sandhills region, a vast expanse of grass-covered dunes.

Visit the Sandhills Wildlife Management Area, a haven for birdwatchers and nature enthusiasts.

Continue to Scottsbluff and explore Scotts Bluff National Monument, which offers stunning views of the surrounding area.

Overnight in Scottsbluff.

Day 6: Chimney Rock and North Platte

Drive to Chimney Rock, an iconic geological formation that played a significant role in the westward expansion.

Proceed to North Platte and visit the Buffalo Bill Ranch State Historical Park to learn about the legendary Buffalo Bill Cody.

If you're interested, stop by the Golden Spike Tower to witness the Union Pacific's Bailey Yard, the largest rail yard in the world.

Overnight in North Platte.

Day 7: Return to Omaha and Departure

Travel back to Omaha for your departure.

Before leaving, explore any attractions or spots you might have missed on your first day.

Bid farewell to Nebraska with wonderful memories and experiences.

Note: This itinerary offers a glimpse of Nebraska's diverse offerings. Depending on your interests, you can customize the trip by including other attractions, such as the Nebraska Sandhills, Agate Fossil Beds National Monument, or the various state parks and recreational areas scattered throughout the state.

CHAPTER 13: TRAVELING NEBRASKA ON A BUDGET

13.1 AFFORDABLE ACCOMMODATION OPTIONS

There are a range of affordable accommodation options for travelers looking to explore Nebraska without breaking the bank. Whether you're visiting the vibrant capital city of Lincoln, the bustling metropolis of Omaha, or the charming small towns and scenic landscapes, there's a place to suit every budget.

For budget-conscious travelers, motels and roadside inns are a popular choice. They offer comfortable rooms and basic amenities at wallet-friendly prices, making them ideal for short stays or those on a road trip.

For a more authentic experience, consider staying in a cozy bed and breakfast. Nebraska boasts numerous charming B&Bs in picturesque settings, where guests can enjoy personalized service and home-cooked breakfasts while immersing themselves in the local culture.

Another affordable option is renting vacation cabins or cottages in the countryside. These provide a tranquil escape and often come with fully equipped kitchens, allowing travelers to save on dining expenses while enjoying the state's natural beauty.

For those who prefer the convenience of a city, budget hotels and hostels can be found in urban centers like Omaha and Lincoln. These accommodations offer a comfortable stay with easy access to local attractions, restaurants, and public transportation.

Lastly, travelers seeking a sense of community and cost-effective lodging might explore Airbnb options. Many homeowners and renters in Nebraska offer rooms or entire apartments at reasonable rates, often with added perks like local tips and insights.

Overall, Nebraska welcomes visitors with open arms and provides a range of affordable accommodation choices, ensuring a memorable stay without stretching the budget.

13.2 FREE AND LOW-COST ATTRACTIONS

For those looking for budget friendly attractions in Nebraska, there are a plethora of free and low-cost attractions that cater to a wide range of interests. Nature enthusiasts can explore the stunning beauty of places like Chimney Rock and Scotts Bluff National Monument, both offering breathtaking vistas and fascinating geological formations.

For history buffs, the Nebraska State Capitol in Lincoln stands tall as a remarkable architectural marvel, with free guided tours available to learn about the state's political heritage. The Strategic Air Command & Aerospace Museum, located near Omaha, offers a glimpse into the history of aviation and space exploration at an affordable entry fee.

In Omaha, the heartwarming Henry Doorly Zoo and Aquarium provides an immersive wildlife experience with a nominal admission fee. The Old Market, a historic district in the city, offers a vibrant atmosphere filled with boutiques, galleries, and restaurants where visitors can wander and enjoy the ambiance.

Art lovers can explore the Joslyn Art Museum in Omaha, showcasing an extensive collection of European and American art, free to the public. Additionally, the Great Platte River Road Archway Monument in Kearney is an interactive museum that chronicles the westward expansion of the United States, with a reasonable entrance fee.

Nebraska's landscape is dotted with numerous parks and recreational areas, like Fontenelle Forest and Mahoney State Park, which provide affordable opportunities for hiking, picnicking, and camping amidst nature's serenity.

Whether it's history, nature, art, or simply enjoying the outdoors, Nebraska offers a wealth of enriching experiences without breaking the bank. Visitors can create cherished memories and gain a deeper appreciation for the state's cultural and natural heritage, all while keeping their expenses in check.

13.3 BUDGET-FRIENDLY DINING

If you find yourself in Nebraska and craving a delicious meal without breaking the bank, worry not, as the state offers an array of budget-friendly dining options. From charming local eateries to cozy diners and family-run restaurants, Nebraska has something to suit every palate and budget.

Indulge in the authentic Midwestern flavors at affordable prices, where farm-to-table dishes showcase the region's bountiful produce. From hearty Nebraska steaks to comforting dishes like Runza (a local specialty) and delectable corn-fed burgers, there's no shortage of tasty, pocket-friendly choices.

Nebraska's welcoming atmosphere extends to its dining scene, with many establishments offering generous portions at modest prices. Whether you're exploring the bustling cities or quaint rural towns, you'll find places that provide a warm ambiance and friendly service without burning a hole in your wallet.

The state's food trucks also add to the charm, serving up diverse and affordable cuisines, making it a perfect choice for a quick and economical bite on the go. Don't forget to treat yourself to homemade pies, a beloved dessert in the area, often served at prices that won't disappoint.

In summary, budget-friendly dining in Nebraska lets you savor the flavors of the heartland without straining your finances. So, come hungry and leave satisfied, as the state's culinary delights promise a delicious and affordable experience for all.

CHAPTER 14: LANGUAGE AND CULTURE

14.1 NEBRASKA'S DIVERSE CULTURE

Nebraska's culture is a beautiful tapestry woven with the threads of various ethnicities, traditions, and histories. Though often associated with its agricultural heritage, the state's cultural landscape is rich and multifaceted, reflecting the contributions of many communities.

The Native American tribes, such as the Omaha, Ponca, and Pawnee, have deep-rooted connections to Nebraska's land and history. Their traditions and customs continue to be celebrated and shared, adding a profound layer of indigenous culture to the state.

Over the years, Nebraska has been a welcoming home to immigrants from across the globe, leading to a vibrant mix of cultures. German, Czech, Irish, Mexican, Vietnamese, Sudanese, and many other communities have settled here, bringing with them their languages, cuisines, music, and festivals. This diversity is particularly evident in urban centers like Omaha and Lincoln, where a myriad of cultural events and international restaurants thrive.

The state's cultural calendar is dotted with numerous celebrations, from the Cinco de Mayo festivities to Oktoberfest and Juneteenth commemorations. These events serve as bridges between communities, fostering a spirit of understanding and appreciation.

Nebraska's cultural diversity has also found expression in its arts and crafts, reflecting both traditional and contemporary styles. Local artisans preserve ancient techniques, while modern artists experiment and create, making the art scene in Nebraska a vibrant and evolving one.

Religion plays a significant role in the lives of Nebraskans, with churches, temples, mosques, and synagogues scattered across the state. This religious diversity adds further depth to the cultural fabric, highlighting the freedom of belief cherished in the region.

Nebraskans take pride in their friendly and welcoming demeanor, valuing the spirit of community and mutual support. This sense of unity has been integral in building bridges between cultures, allowing for harmonious coexistence and exchange of ideas.

Overall, Nebraska's diverse culture stands as a testament to the richness that emerges when people from various backgrounds come together, share, and celebrate their unique identities while contributing to the collective identity of the state. It is a reminder that unity in diversity is not just a slogan but a lived reality, making Nebraska a fascinating and inclusive place to call home.

14.2 LOCAL CUSTOMS AND ETIQUETTE

In Nebraska, local customs and etiquette reflect the state's warm and friendly nature, rooted in Midwestern hospitality. When visiting the Cornhusker State, it's essential to observe these customs to ensure a positive and respectful experience:

Greetings: Nebraskans are known for their warm greetings and friendly smiles. A firm handshake or a simple wave is customary when meeting someone for the first time.

Politeness: Politeness and courtesy are highly valued in Nebraska. Saying "please" and "thank you" is expected in all interactions, whether it's at a restaurant, store, or someone's home.

Respect for personal space: Nebraskans appreciate their personal space, so maintain an appropriate distance when conversing with others.

Punctuality: Being on time for appointments, meetings, or social gatherings is considered a sign of respect for others' time.

Eye contact: Maintaining eye contact while speaking shows sincerity and interest in the conversation.

Gift-giving: If invited to someone's home, bringing a small gift, such as a bouquet of flowers or a local specialty, is a thoughtful gesture.

Dining etiquette: During meals, wait for the host to say grace or start eating before you begin. Keep your elbows off the table and use utensils properly.

Conversation topics: Nebraskans enjoy discussing sports, weather, agriculture, and local events. Avoid controversial topics or sensitive issues unless brought up by your host.

Dress code: Casual and comfortable attire is generally suitable for most occasions, but it's always best to check the dress code for specific events.

Tipping: It is customary to leave a 15-20% tip for servers at restaurants, as it is an essential part of their income.

Holding doors: Holding doors open for others, regardless of gender, is a common courtesy.

Driving etiquette: Nebraskans are generally polite drivers who follow traffic rules. Use your turn signals, maintain a safe following distance, and yield to others when appropriate.

Weather conversations: Weather is a popular topic in Nebraska, given its variable climate. Engaging in weather-related discussions is a great icebreaker.

RSVP: When invited to an event, promptly respond to the invitation, indicating whether you will attend or not.

Thank-you notes: Sending a handwritten thank-you note after a social gathering or when receiving a gift is a thoughtful gesture.

By respecting these local customs and etiquette, you will undoubtedly find yourself embraced by the warmth and friendliness of the people of Nebraska, making your experience in the state all the more enjoyable.

14.3 LEARNING BASIC PHRASES IN NEBRASKA

For travelers visiting Nebraska, it's always helpful to know some basic phrases to ease communication and enhance your overall experience. While English is widely spoken throughout the state, incorporating a few Nebraska-specific phrases can be a great way to connect with locals and show your appreciation for their culture. Here are some essential phrases to get you started:

"**Howdy**": A traditional Nebraskan greeting that means "hello." This friendly and informal term is commonly used throughout the state.

"**Ya betcha!**": An enthusiastic affirmation meaning "yes" or "absolutely." Nebraskans often use this phrase to express agreement or show their enthusiasm.

"**Cornhuskers**": Refers to the University of Nebraska's sports teams. It's an essential term for any Nebraska sports-related conversation.

"The Good Life": Nebraska's state slogan, representing the state's reputation for its high quality of life and friendly communities.

"Where's the nearest Runza?": A Runza is a famous Nebraska-based fast-food chain known for its signature dish, the "Runza sandwich" filled with beef, cabbage, and onions. It's a must-try while in the state.

"Tornado Alley": A colloquial term used to describe the region where Nebraska is situated, which is prone to tornadoes during certain times of the year.

"Corny": An adjective often used by Nebraskans to describe something that is quirky, outdated, or filled with rural charm.

"The Sandhills": Refers to the Sandhills region in Nebraska, known for its unique landscape and large sand dunes.

"Steak": Nebraskans are proud of their beef, so if you're looking for a delicious meal, ask for recommendations on where to find the best steak in town.

"Husking": The process of removing the husk from corn. It's a significant activity in Nebraska and often associated with fun events like corn husking contests.

"Flatlander": A term used to describe someone from a region without many hills or mountains, such as those from the eastern United States.

"Big Red": Another term referring to the University of Nebraska Cornhuskers, particularly their football team.

"Chimney Rock": A famous landmark in Nebraska, historically significant for pioneers traveling along the Oregon Trail.

"Omaha" and "Lincoln": The two largest cities in Nebraska, known for their distinct cultures and attractions.

"Kool-Aid": Nebraska is the birthplace of this iconic powdered drink mix, and it's still popular among locals.

Remember, while these phrases can add a local touch to your conversations, most Nebraskans will readily communicate in standard English.

Being polite and respectful will always be appreciated, and don't hesitate to strike up a conversation with friendly Nebraskans - they are known for their warm hospitality and welcoming nature!

CHAPTER 15: NEBRASKA SOUVENIRS AND MEMENTOS

15.1 UNIQUE GIFTS TO BRING HOME

Here are some must-take-home goodies that would keep your memories about Nebraska alive:

Handcrafted Pottery: Nebraska is home to many talented potters who create unique and beautiful ceramic pieces. Bring home a handcrafted vase, bowl, or mug that reflects the state's artistic flair.

Corn Husk Dolls: Corn Husk dolls are a traditional Native American craft that has a deep connection to Nebraska's history. These charming dolls make for a distinctive and culturally significant gift.

Sandhill Crane Art: Nebraska's Platte River is a renowned migration site for Sandhill cranes. Celebrate this natural wonder with artwork or sculptures depicting these graceful birds.

Buffalo Jerky: Buffalo jerky is a delicious and exotic treat that captures the essence of Nebraska's Great Plains. It's a perfect gift for food enthusiasts or those seeking a unique taste experience.

Arbor Day Trees: Nebraska is the birthplace of Arbor Day, and it's an excellent opportunity to bring home a tree seedling or sapling to plant and commemorate your trip.

Nebraska Wine: Surprise your loved ones with a bottle of locally produced wine from one of Nebraska's burgeoning vineyards. The unique climate and soil give these wines a distinct character.

Kool-Aid Products: Kool-Aid was invented in Hastings, Nebraska, and you can find an array of Kool-Aid merchandise and souvenirs that would delight both kids and adults alike.

Handwoven Rugs: Nebraska is known for its skilled weavers who create stunning, handwoven rugs and tapestries. A rug showcasing Nebraska's landscapes would be a cherished gift.

Historic Pioneer Books: Explore the history of Nebraska's pioneers through books and novels that vividly narrate the tales of the past.

Sunflower-Themed Gifts: As the "Cornhusker State," sunflowers are a common sight in Nebraska. Bring home sunflower-themed items like paintings, mugs, or even sunflower seed packets.

Homestead National Monument Souvenirs: Commemorate your visit to the Homestead National Monument with souvenirs that reflect the struggles and triumphs of early settlers.

Vintage Postcards: Seek out vintage postcards featuring iconic Nebraska landmarks and scenic vistas. They make for nostalgic and unique keepsakes.

Handmade Soap: Artisanal soaps crafted with natural ingredients can be found in many

Nebraska gift shops. They offer a refreshing and fragrant reminder of your journey.

Nebraska Shaped Jewelry: Look for jewelry designed in the shape of Nebraska, such as necklaces or bracelets, to carry a piece of the state with you.

Local Honey: Nebraska boasts diverse landscapes, making it an excellent place for bees to produce delicious honey. Bringing home a jar of locally sourced honey supports local beekeepers and delights taste buds.

Farm Fresh Goodies: Stop by a local farmers' market and pick up fresh produce, jams, or baked goods from Nebraska's fertile farmlands.

Customized Cornhole Boards: Cornhole is a popular lawn game in Nebraska, and you can find unique cornhole boards with custom designs and themes.

Petrified Wood Artifacts: Some regions of Nebraska have deposits of ancient petrified wood. Bring home a polished petrified wood piece or a crafted artifact as a one-of-a-kind gift.

Western-style Leather Goods: Embrace the Western spirit with leather belts, wallets, or accessories crafted by skilled artisans in the state.

Wind Chimes: Choose wind chimes inspired by Nebraska's natural elements, such as prairie grass or sandhill cranes, to add a touch of soothing melody to any space.

These unique gifts from Nebraska will not only remind you of your memorable trip but also make thoughtful presents for family and friends.

15.2 LOCAL ART AND HANDICRAFTS

Nebraska is a state with a rich cultural heritage that cherishes its local art and handicrafts. Embodying the spirit of the Midwest, Nebraska's artisans and craftspeople produce a diverse array of unique creations that reflect the state's natural beauty and vibrant history.

From the bustling cities to the serene countryside, local art can be found in galleries, craft fairs, and community events throughout Nebraska. Traditional crafts such as quilting, pottery, and woodworking are passed down through generations, keeping the spirit of craftsmanship alive. These cherished pieces not only serve as decorative items but also represent the strong sense of community and family ties within the state.

In addition to the traditional crafts, Nebraska's local art scene embraces contemporary expressions, with a burgeoning community of painters, sculptors, and mixed media artists. Drawing inspiration from the vast prairies, rolling hills, and iconic landmarks like Chimney Rock and Scotts Bluff, their creations capture the essence of Nebraska's landscapes and its ever-changing seasons.

Moreover, the state's Native American heritage plays a significant role in influencing its art and handicrafts. Traditional tribal designs, beadwork, and exquisite pottery pay homage to the ancestral wisdom and artistic legacy of Nebraska's indigenous people.

Nebraska also boasts a thriving community of local artisans who take inspiration from urban life and modern culture. From handmade jewelry to upcycled fashion, their innovative creations blend contemporary aesthetics with a touch of Nebraska's down-to-earth charm.

The appreciation for local art and handicrafts in Nebraska extends beyond the borders of the state. Tourists and visitors are drawn to the genuine craftsmanship and unique designs, making it a popular destination for art enthusiasts and collectors alike.

In conclusion, Nebraska's local art and handicrafts reflect the state's distinct identity, encapsulating its history, natural beauty, and diverse cultural influences. Whether it's a beautifully woven quilt, a masterfully carved wooden sculpture, or a contemporary painting inspired by the prairie skies, Nebraska's artistic community continues to thrive, preserving its heritage while embracing the future.

15.3 WHERE TO SHOP FOR SOUVENIRS

When you visit Nebraska, you'll find a variety of unique souvenirs that reflect the state's rich history, culture, and natural beauty. Whether you're exploring the vibrant cities or the picturesque countryside, here are some fantastic places to shop for souvenirs in Nebraska:

Old Market District (Omaha): Located in downtown Omaha, the Old Market District is a popular shopping destination with an abundance of charming boutiques, art galleries, and specialty shops. Here, you can find locally-made arts and crafts, Nebraska-themed apparel, and handcrafted jewelry, all perfect for souvenirs.

Haymarket District (Lincoln): Similar to the Old Market in Omaha, Lincoln's Haymarket District offers a diverse selection of souvenir shops. From vintage stores to contemporary boutiques, you'll discover everything from Huskers-themed memorabilia to artisanal products representing Nebraska's agricultural heritage.

Nebraska State Capitol Gift Shop (Lincoln): Inside the magnificent Nebraska State Capitol, you'll find a gift shop that showcases a wide range of Nebraska-centric souvenirs. From postcards and books detailing the state's history to unique items featuring the capitol building's design, this shop is an excellent stop for politically and historically inclined visitors.

Carhenge Gift Shop (Alliance): Carhenge, a quirky and fascinating roadside attraction in Alliance, Nebraska, offers a gift shop with an array of fun and unusual souvenirs. You'll find Carhenge-themed t-shirts, mugs, keychains, and more, making it a must-visit spot for offbeat souvenirs.

Strategic Air Command & Aerospace Museum (Ashland): For aviation enthusiasts, this museum's gift shop is a treasure trove of aerospace-related souvenirs. From model aircraft to astronaut-themed memorabilia, you can take home a piece of Nebraska's aerospace history.

Fort Cody Trading Post (North Platte): This iconic trading post is designed to resemble an old frontier fort and offers a mix of Western and Native American-themed souvenirs. You can find cowboy hats, Native American jewelry, and Nebraska-themed collectibles that embody the state's Western heritage.

Scotts Bluff National Monument Visitor Center (Gering): The Visitor Center at Scotts Bluff National Monument features a gift shop with souvenirs reflecting the natural beauty and historical significance of the region. Look for items like National Park memorabilia, books about the Oregon Trail, and Native American crafts.

Unique Small Town Shops: As you explore the smaller towns and communities across Nebraska, keep an eye out for local gift shops and artisan boutiques. These hidden gems often offer one-of-a-kind souvenirs, including handmade crafts, locally-produced food items, and distinctive artwork.

Remember, Nebraska's souvenirs encompass a wide range of themes, from the state's agricultural heritage and Wild West history to its beautiful landscapes and modern cultural identity. Take your time exploring various shops to find the perfect memento that resonates with your experience of the Cornhusker State.

CONCLUSION

This travel guidebook has endeavored to showcase the myriad wonders and hidden gems that Nebraska has to offer. Throughout its pages, we have strived to provide an enriching and insightful experience for travelers seeking to explore the heart of America's Great Plains.

Our guidebook has been meticulously crafted to present a wealth of valuable information, allowing readers to embark on an unforgettable journey through Nebraska's diverse landscapes, vibrant culture, and captivating history. From the rolling sandhills and vast prairies to the bustling cities and tranquil small towns, we have covered every corner of this remarkable state.

Within these pages, travelers have discovered an array of must-visit destinations, from the iconic landmarks like Chimney Rock and Scotts Bluff National Monument to the lesser-known treasures such as the Sandhill Crane migration in Kearney and the quirky Carhenge in Alliance. We have provided insightful recommendations on exploring the vibrant arts scene in Omaha, experiencing the agricultural heritage in Grand Island, and immersing in the rich Native American history in Scottsbluff.

Furthermore, our guidebook has been dedicated to assisting travelers in planning their itineraries with comprehensive information on accommodations, dining options, transportation, and various recreational activities. By offering practical tips and local insights, we have sought to ensure that visitors can make the most of their time in Nebraska, creating unforgettable memories that will last a lifetime.

As Nebraska continues to evolve and grow, this guidebook aims to remain a timeless companion for travelers seeking an authentic and rewarding experience in this charming Midwestern state. Whether you are an adventurous spirit, a history enthusiast, a nature lover, or a connoisseur of culture, we believe that Nebraska has something special to offer you, and we hope that this guidebook has been an invaluable tool in facilitating your journey.

With the profound beauty of the prairies, the warmth of its people, and the rich tapestry of its heritage, Nebraska stands as a testament to the essence of American heartland charm. As you set off on your own Nebraska adventure, may this guidebook be your steadfast companion, inspiring you to forge a deep connection with the land, its people, and the timeless spirit that embodies this captivating state. Safe travels and bon voyage!

Printed in Great Britain
by Amazon

45043090R00145